AI Implementation Blind Spots

How to Make AI Adoption Work in Real Business Systems

A Decision-First Field Manual for Reducing Rework, Controlling Risk, and Turning AI Speed Into Measurable Results

Author: Nikolay Gul

Publisher: Future-Proof Marketing Press
Printed in the United States of America.

Copyright

Disclaimer

This book is provided for educational, informational, and strategic planning purposes only. It does not provide legal, financial, accounting, investment, cybersecurity, healthcare, compliance, insurance, employment, procurement, or regulatory advice.

Readers should consult qualified professionals before making decisions that affect regulated operations, employee roles, financial reporting, customer data, cybersecurity response, healthcare administration, legal exposure, insurance coverage, contracts, compliance obligations, or investment decisions.

Artificial intelligence capabilities, vendors, laws, standards, regulations, platform rules, and industry practices change quickly. The principles in this book are designed to remain useful across changing tools, but specific technical, legal, financial, security, operational, and regulatory details should always be verified against current sources and professional guidance.

The examples, modeled scenarios, calculations, scorecards, and case studies in this book are provided for planning and educational purposes. Unless specifically stated otherwise, they are modeled examples, not audited client results, legal opinions, financial projections, or guarantees of performance.

No business outcome, cost reduction, revenue improvement, margin improvement, risk reduction, productivity gain, cybersecurity improvement, compliance result, or operational improvement is guaranteed by using the concepts in this book. Results depend on the organization, workflow, data quality, risk level, implementation discipline, governance, tooling, human oversight, and operating context.

Readers are responsible for their own judgment, professional review, and implementation decisions.

Contents

How to Use This Book

This book is a field manual, not a motivational book about artificial intelligence.

It was written for readers who need to make AI adoption work inside real business systems: executives, founders, AI strategists, consultants, MSP leaders, cybersecurity professionals, finance teams, operations leaders, marketers, GTM teams, compliance leaders, and implementation teams.

The book has one central argument:

AI does not create business value merely because it produces output faster. AI creates value when it improves real workflows, real decisions, real ownership, real evidence, real economics, and real risk control.

You do not need to read this book only from front to back, although that is the best path for first-time readers.

Part I explains the blind spots that make AI adoption look better than it really is: speed without value, activity without ownership, hidden rework, pilots that do not scale, and AI-influenced decisions without accountability.

Part II reframes AI strategy around decisions instead of tools. This is where the book defines the AI Strategist as a Decision Architect and explains why financial translation matters.

Part III provides the core operating system: workflow mapping, bottleneck prioritization, decision boundaries, workflow design, pilot proof, and scale-or-stop discipline.

Part IV translates the system into enterprise domains: revenue, operations, finance, and high-risk environments such as cybersecurity, healthcare administration, and regulated AI.

Part V provides compact hard-dollar case studies. These are designed to show how the same blind spots appear in MSPs, cybersecurity, marketing, finance, and executive reporting.

Part VI gives practical tools that can be used in meetings, pilots, workshops, consulting engagements, and internal AI reviews.

Readers who are executives may want to focus first on Chapters 1, 3, 4, 8, 11, 14, and Part V.

Readers who are AI strategists or consultants may want to focus on Chapters 6, 7, 9, 11, 13, 14, and Part VI.

Readers in cybersecurity, compliance, finance, healthcare administration, or regulated environments should pay special attention to Chapters 5, 11, 12, 17, and 18.

Readers in marketing, sales, GTM, customer success, and service delivery should focus on Chapters 1, 6, 8, 15, and the relevant case studies.

The book is designed to be practical. Mark it up. Use the questions. Bring the tools into meetings. Challenge your own AI initiatives against the frameworks.

The goal is not to slow AI down.

The goal is to make AI speed useful.

Note on Examples, Calculations, and Source Claims

The examples and case studies in this book are designed to teach implementation logic. Unless clearly stated otherwise, they are modeled scenarios for planning purposes, not audited client results.

The calculations in this book are practical decision tools. They are not formal accounting models, financial audits, legal standards, cybersecurity frameworks, compliance determinations, or statistical guarantees.

For example, the Rework Tax and Real Velocity formulas are intended to help teams ask better questions:

What happens after AI produces the first output?
How much verification is still required?
How much correction remains?
How often do exceptions appear?
How quickly are errors detected?
Does the workflow still improve after hidden work is counted?

These questions matter because AI implementation often fails in the gap between visible output and trusted usable work.

The external research discussed in this book should also be used carefully. Industry reports about AI pilots, agentic AI, ROI, and enterprise adoption are useful warning signals, not universal laws. They should not be read as proof that AI is failing. They should be read as evidence that AI adoption and AI implementation are not the same thing.

AI can create real value. But it creates durable value only when organizations connect tools to workflows, decisions, owners, boundaries, evidence, economics, and risk controls.

That is the discipline this book is built around.

Companion Resources Note

This book includes compact tools, templates, scorecards, and checklists inside Part VI.

Extended versions may be made available through the companion resource page:

AiStrategyService.com

Companion resources may include editable worksheets, expanded calculators, implementation prompts, workshop templates, case-study extensions, source-note updates, and practical materials for teams, consultants, AI strategists, and business leaders.

The printed book is intentionally designed as a field manual, not a full workbook. The companion resources are intended to help readers apply the ideas without making the paperback unnecessarily large.

For the most current companion materials, source updates, and implementation resources, visit:

AiStrategyService.com

PART I - THE PROBLEM NO ONE MEASURES
Chapter 1 - The Velocity Trap and AI Brain Fry

Why Speed Does Not Equal Value

The executive meeting started well.

The company had adopted several AI tools across sales, marketing, customer support, operations, and IT. The early numbers looked impressive. Sales reps were writing follow-up emails faster. Marketing was producing campaign drafts in minutes. Support agents were summarizing tickets in seconds. Analysts were generating reports before lunch that used to take two days.

Managers were excited.

The board liked the story.

Then the COO asked the question nobody had prepared for.

"Are we actually better?"

The room went quiet.

The sales leader said the team was sending more emails, but response quality was uneven. The marketing director said content volume had doubled, but the best customers were starting to ignore it. The support manager said ticket summaries were faster, but senior agents were spending more time checking them. The CTO said developers were moving faster, but pull requests were getting harder to review. The CFO asked whether headcount, margin, cycle time, customer retention, error rates, or customer satisfaction had improved.

No one had a clean answer.

The organization had measured AI activity.

It had not measured AI value.

That is the Velocity Trap.

AI made the work faster, but the business system did not become clearer. Decisions did not become better. Ownership did not become sharper. Risk did not become easier to manage. The company had more output, more movement, and more confidence — but not necessarily more business value.

This is the first blind spot:

Organizations often measure how much faster AI creates output, but not how much harder the business must work to trust, use, and govern that output.

Most organizations think the AI implementation problem is a software problem.

It is not.

It is a decision design problem.

Software can generate drafts, summaries, code, reports, recommendations, and workflow suggestions. But business value begins after the output appears. Someone must decide whether that output is correct, useful, safe, relevant, compliant, profitable, and appropriate for the customer or situation.

When that decision layer is missing, AI speed can become a cost.

The organization gets faster at creating things humans must inspect.

That is not transformation.

That is an output factory with a review bottleneck.

The Velocity Trap

The Velocity Trap happens when AI increases the speed of output faster than the organization increases its ability to evaluate, control, and use that output.

The visible gain is speed.

The hidden cost is review.

The deeper cost is cognitive load.

The most dangerous cost is false confidence.

AI does not merely increase output. It increases the number of decisions humans must make about output.

Is this correct?

Is this complete?

Is this safe?

Is this aligned with the customer?

Is this legally acceptable?

Is this useful enough to send, ship, approve, automate, or scale?

When those questions are not built into the workflow, humans become the shock absorbers of AI adoption. They absorb ambiguity, risk, review pressure, exception handling, and the fear of missing something important.

Eventually, the system feels faster from the outside but heavier from the inside.

That is the first implementation law of this book:

Speed without boundaries creates cost.

Faster Feels Like Better

Speed is seductive because it is visible.

A manager can see an AI-generated report appear in ten seconds. A salesperson can see five email drafts instead of one. A marketing team can produce twenty headline options before the meeting starts. A support agent can summarize a long ticket thread instantly.

The improvement feels obvious.

Before AI: slow.

After AI: fast.

But speed is only one part of value.

A faster bad answer is not a better answer. A faster unclear proposal is not a better proposal. A faster unreviewed customer response is not better service. A faster invoice classification that requires manual cleanup is not better finance. A faster security recommendation without ownership is not better protection.

AI speed is real. The mistake is assuming speed automatically becomes margin, quality, trust, capacity, or strategic advantage.

It does not.

Speed must pass through a business filter:

Did AI reduce real work, or did it move the work somewhere else?

Many organizations do not ask that question early enough. They count generated outputs, not validated outcomes. They count usage, not decision quality. They count adoption, not business improvement.

This is why AI can look successful during the demo and become expensive during implementation.

In the demo, AI produces.

In the business system, AI must fit.

Those are different problems.

The Business Does Not Pay for Output

Business leaders often say they want productivity.

What they usually mean is not "more things."

They want useful results with less waste: shorter cycle times, lower cost per unit, fewer defects, better customer experience, cleaner handoffs, fewer escalations, and more capacity without uncontrolled risk.

AI output only matters when it improves one or more of those outcomes.

A 30-page AI-generated report is not value if no one trusts it.

A list of 500 sales prospects is not value if the fit is poor.

A code block is not value if it increases maintenance burden.

A chatbot response is not value if it creates customer confusion.

A compliance summary is not value if legal still needs to redo it.

A support classification is not value if a senior technician must reopen every ticket.

The business does not pay for raw AI output. The business pays for usable decisions, completed work, reduced risk, improved throughput, better customer outcomes, and measurable financial impact.

That is why AI implementation must begin with decisions, not tools.

A tool-first organization asks:

"Can AI do this task?"

A decision-first organization asks:

"What decision does this task support, who owns that decision, what evidence is required, and what happens if AI is wrong?"

The first question produces experiments.

The second question produces implementation discipline.

AI Brain Fry

Some teams informally describe a new kind of work fatigue as AI Brain Fry.

The phrase is informal, but the problem is real.

AI Brain Fry happens when humans must evaluate too many machine-generated options, drafts, summaries, predictions, recommendations, and exceptions without clear decision rules.

It is not ordinary burnout from doing too much work.

It is cognitive fatigue from supervising output at machine speed.

A person can write one report and understand the assumptions behind it. But if AI generates ten versions, the person must compare them, detect mistakes, judge tone, evaluate missing context, choose the best version, and worry about what was overlooked.

A support agent can read one customer thread and understand the issue. But if AI summarizes fifty ticket histories, the agent must decide which summaries are accurate enough to trust.

A marketing manager can review one campaign draft carefully. But if the team generates forty ad variations, the manager must sort through a pile of plausible mediocrity.

A developer can review code written by a teammate and ask questions. But AI-generated code may arrive quickly, confidently, and without the reasoning trail a human reviewer needs.

This is not always faster.

Sometimes it is mentally more expensive.

The employee is no longer only doing the old task. The employee is doing the old task, plus AI supervision, plus error detection, plus exception judgment, plus reputational risk management.

If the workflow is not redesigned, AI does not remove work.

It changes the shape of work.

Sometimes that is useful.

Sometimes it is risky.

Sometimes it simply hides the cost.

From Doing Work to Validating Work

Many AI adoption plans assume the human will do less.

In practice, the human often does something different.

Before AI, the human created the work product.

After AI, the human validates the work product.

That can be a real improvement, but only if the validation burden is smaller than the creation burden.

If a support agent used to spend eight minutes reading a ticket and writing a response, and AI reduces that to three minutes with reliable quality, the gain is real.

But if AI produces a draft in thirty seconds and the agent spends six minutes checking facts, fixing tone, correcting account details, and verifying policy, the gain is smaller than it appears.

The organization celebrates the speed of generation.

The worker experiences the burden of verification.

Both stories can be true.

The mistake is choosing one story and ignoring the other.

This is why "AI saved us time" is not enough.

The better question is:

"After review, correction, and exception handling, did the workflow still improve?"

That question becomes central later in this book. For now, the point is simpler:

AI speed is useful only when the business can absorb, trust, and act on the output without creating a larger hidden burden.

In Practice: MSP Ticket Triage

Consider a managed service provider that adopts AI to help triage support tickets.

The goal sounds reasonable. Tickets arrive all day. Some are password resets. Some are printer issues. Some are endpoint alerts. Some are suspicious login events. Some are urgent outages.

If AI can summarize tickets, classify severity, suggest routing, and draft replies, the MSP should become faster.

In the first month, the numbers look good. Average initial ticket summary time drops. The team processes more tickets per hour. The service manager sees improved dashboard activity. The tool appears successful.

Then the hidden problem appears.

Senior technicians begin checking the AI summaries because some miss important context.

A ticket marked "routine access issue" turns out to involve a terminated employee account.

A "slow computer" ticket includes signs of possible malware activity.

A "printer issue" is really a network segmentation problem affecting multiple users.

A "user cannot log in" ticket is related to a conditional access policy change.

The AI did not fail completely. It helped.

But it did not understand the MSP's operating context.

It did not know which signals required escalation. It did not know when a simple support issue might indicate security risk. It did not know which clients had special contractual requirements. It did not know which users were executives. It did not know the difference between a normal issue and an issue that looked normal but carried business risk.

So the senior technicians became the real triage system.

The AI made the first pass faster.

The humans carried the judgment burden.

This is the Velocity Trap in operational form.

A weak implementation would say:

"The AI tool is not accurate enough."

A better implementation would say:

"We did not define the decision properly."

Ticket triage is not one decision. It is several decisions stacked together.

What is the issue? How urgent is it? Who is affected? What system is involved? Is there security exposure? Is there business downtime? Does the client contract change the response requirement? Can AI route this automatically, or should it recommend a route? When must a human review the classification? When must the issue escalate?

Without these rules, the AI tool is asked to guess inside a business system it does not fully understand.

That is not implementation.

That is delegation without architecture.

A better MSP workflow would let AI summarize tickets, extract affected systems, identify missing information, suggest severity, and flag possible escalation triggers. But it would clearly define which classifications AI can make alone, which require technician review, and which must be escalated immediately.

Now AI has a role.

The human has a role.

The workflow has a rule.

The business can measure whether the system is actually improving.

That is the difference between speed and implementation.

In Practice: Marketing Content Inflation

Marketing teams are especially vulnerable to the Velocity Trap because generative AI is visibly good at producing language.

It can write emails, ads, landing pages, blog outlines, social posts, webinar descriptions, product copy, executive summaries, buyer personas, call scripts, and competitive comparisons.

For a busy marketing team, this feels like oxygen.

The team that once struggled to produce five campaign ideas can now produce fifty.

At first, this feels like a breakthrough.

Then the second-order problems arrive.

The copy starts sounding similar. The claims become polished but generic. The personalization becomes shallow. The sales team complains that prospects have "heard this already." The CEO likes the volume but questions the substance. Customers begin ignoring the emails. The company publishes more but says less.

The marketing dashboard shows activity.

The market shows indifference.

The team solved the production problem but not the trust problem.

Marketing does not win because it says more.

It wins because it says something specific, credible, timely, relevant, and believable to the right buyer.

AI can help with that. But only when the team gives it strategy, evidence, constraints, customer insight, differentiation, and review discipline.

Without those, AI becomes a content inflation machine.

A content inflation machine creates the illusion of marketing productivity while increasing the burden on brand trust.

The problem is not that AI wrote the draft. The problem is that no one defined the decision the draft was supposed to support.

Was the email supposed to create a meeting?

Was the article supposed to educate a skeptical buyer?

Was the case study supposed to reduce perceived risk?

Was the landing page supposed to qualify demand?

Was the campaign supposed to differentiate the company from competitors?

If the decision is unclear, the output becomes decorative.

Good AI marketing implementation does not start with "write ten emails."

It starts with:

"What buyer decision are we trying to influence, what proof does that buyer need, what claim can we honestly make, what risk must we avoid, and how will we know if trust increased or decreased?"

Now AI has a job.

Not to produce words.

To support a buyer decision.

That is a different standard.

Why "Human in the Loop" Is Not Enough

Many organizations respond to AI risk with the phrase "human in the loop."

That sounds responsible.

Sometimes it is.

But by itself, it is incomplete.

Which human?

At what point in the workflow?

With what authority?

Using what standard?

Reviewing what evidence?

Responsible for what outcome?

Allowed to override what?

Required to document what?

Escalating to whom?

Measured how?

A vague human in the loop often becomes a human in the blame path.

The organization says AI is supervised. In practice, an overworked employee clicks approve because the system gives them too much output and too little context.

That is not governance.

That is liability with a checkbox.

A useful human-in-the-loop design must specify the human, the timing, the authority, the review standard, the evidence, and the escalation path.

Otherwise, the human becomes a rubber stamp or a bottleneck.

Neither is a serious implementation model.

This does not mean every AI workflow needs heavy governance. Low-risk internal brainstorming does not need the same controls as financial approval, cybersecurity response, healthcare administration, or customer-facing commitments.

But the level of control should match the level of risk.

If AI influences a decision that affects money, customers, security, compliance, employees, or reputation, the human role must be clear enough to be useful.

"Human in the loop" is not a strategy.

It is a starting point.

What the CFO Sees

The AI enthusiast sees speed.

The CFO sees cost behavior.

Both perspectives matter.

If AI reduces time per task but increases review time, exception handling, quality control, tool cost, integration cost, training cost, legal review, customer recovery, or management overhead, the financial story changes.

This does not mean AI is bad.

It means AI must be measured honestly.

A CFO does not need every AI project to produce immediate profit. Some projects create learning, resilience, capacity, or strategic options. But the CFO does need clarity about what kind of value is being pursued and what cost is being introduced.

The Velocity Trap becomes dangerous when AI costs hide under enthusiasm.

The tool subscription is visible.

The review burden is less visible.

The cloud cost may be visible.

The exception handling is less visible.

The vendor invoice is visible.

The brand risk is less visible.

The productivity claim is visible.

The rework is less visible.

A practical planning question is:

"After humans review, correct, and manage exceptions, is the workflow still better?"

If the answer is yes, AI may be creating real value.

If the answer is unclear, the organization does not yet have implementation evidence.

If the answer is no, the organization may have bought speed and inherited complexity.

This is not a finance objection to AI.

It is a finance demand for reality.

Good AI strategy should welcome that demand.

A project that cannot survive honest measurement probably should not scale.

The Real Promise of AI Speed

This chapter is not an argument against AI speed.

It is an argument for using AI speed properly.

AI speed is valuable when it removes friction from well-designed decisions. It is valuable when it gives humans better evidence. It is valuable when it reduces low-value manual effort. It is valuable when it improves response time without weakening trust. It is valuable when it helps experts see patterns faster. It is valuable when it helps teams scale quality, not just volume.

That is the future worth building.

Not AI as a magic replacement for judgment.

Not AI as a content machine.

Not AI as a vendor slogan.

Not AI as a pile of pilots.

AI as disciplined acceleration inside real business systems.

The companies that benefit most from AI will not necessarily be the ones that produce the most output. They will be the ones that connect AI speed to better decisions, clearer ownership, controlled risk, and measurable outcomes.

That is why this book begins here.

The first blind spot is speed itself.

Speed feels like progress.

But in real business systems, speed only matters when it moves the right decision, through the right control, toward the right outcome.

Everything else is motion.

Decision Architect's Field Notes

What to Do Next

Identify one AI use case already active in your organization. Do not start with the most exciting one. Start with the one people are already using.

Write down the business workflow it touches.

Then answer four questions:

What output does AI create?

Who reviews or uses that output?

What decision does that output support?

What happens if the output is wrong, incomplete, generic, or misapplied?

If the team cannot answer those questions clearly, the use case is not yet implementation-ready. It may still be useful, but it needs a clearer decision structure before it deserves scale.

For a practical first exercise, choose one workflow and mark each AI activity as one of the following:

Assist

Recommend

Act

Escalate

Stop

This simple classification will expose more implementation risk than a long strategy meeting.

Common Traps to Avoid

Do not treat faster output as proof of business value.

Do not assume "human in the loop" is meaningful unless the human, timing, authority, evidence, and escalation rules are defined.

Do not let AI turn experts into exhausted reviewers of machine-generated material.

Do not measure usage alone. Usage tells you people are touching the tool. It does not tell you whether the system improved.

Do not automate unclear decisions. AI will not repair a workflow the organization itself does not understand.

Do not scale a pilot because the demo looked impressive. Scale only when the workflow has evidence, ownership, boundaries, and measurable improvement after review and correction.

Boardroom Question

Where are we currently measuring AI speed while failing to measure review burden, exception cost, decision quality, and business outcome?

Industry Translation

For MSPs, the Velocity Trap appears when AI summarizes and routes tickets faster, but senior technicians still carry the real judgment burden.

For cybersecurity teams, it appears when AI accelerates alert summaries but does not clarify severity, escalation, or response ownership.

For marketing and GTM teams, it appears when AI increases content volume while weakening differentiation, trust, and buyer relevance.

For finance teams, it appears when AI classifies documents or invoices faster but exceptions still require manual cleanup and risk review.

For healthcare administrators, it appears when AI drafts communications faster but accuracy, privacy, and role boundaries remain unclear.

For executives and boards, it appears when AI adoption dashboards show activity but not margin, quality, risk reduction, customer impact, or enterprise-level value.

Implementation Law

Speed without boundaries creates cost.

Chapter 2 - AI Theater vs. the AI Implementation Studio

Why Adoption Activity Is Not Implementation

The executive update looked impressive.

Every department had something to report.

Marketing was using AI to draft articles, email campaigns, social posts, and webinar descriptions. Sales was testing AI-generated prospecting messages. Customer support was using AI for ticket summaries. Finance was experimenting with invoice classification. Cybersecurity was testing alert summaries. HR had rewritten job descriptions. IT had approved several new tools. A few employees had built prompt libraries. A few managers had become internal AI champions.

The slide looked clean.

The message sounded confident.

AI adoption is active across the company.

Then the CFO asked a plain question.

"What business result changed?"

The room became less comfortable.

Marketing had more content, but no clear increase in qualified pipeline. Sales had more messages, but no reliable improvement in meetings. Support had faster ticket summaries, but escalation rates had not improved. Finance had tested invoice classification, but exceptions still required manual review. IT had more AI requests, but no complete picture of tool cost, data exposure, workflow ownership, or risk. Cybersecurity liked the faster summaries, but analysts still did not trust AI enough to let it influence response decisions.

The company had activity.

It did not yet have implementation.

That is AI Theater.

AI Theater happens when an organization performs AI adoption through pilots, demos, tool usage, training sessions, announcements, dashboards, and internal excitement without changing the decisions, ownership, workflows, risk controls, and measurement systems around the work.

Most AI Theater is not dishonest. It is usually created by good intentions moving faster than business discipline.

Leaders want momentum. Employees want better tools. Vendors promise acceleration. Boards ask what the company is doing with AI. Competitors talk about transformation. Nobody wants to look behind.

So the company starts moving.

But movement is not the same as implementation.

The blind spot is this:

Organizations often mistake visible AI activity for real AI implementation.

That mistake is expensive because activity is easy to celebrate and hard to challenge.

Implementation asks a harder question:

What changed in the business system?

Adoption Is Not Implementation

Adoption means people are using AI.

Implementation means AI has been built into a real workflow in a way that improves a defined business outcome.

Those two ideas are connected, but they are not the same.

Adoption can be measured by logins, licenses, training attendance, prompts submitted, documents generated, meetings summarized, features enabled, or pilots launched.

Implementation must be measured by stronger evidence: shorter cycle time, lower cost per unit, fewer errors, better customer response, improved conversion, cleaner handoffs, reduced rework, faster resolution, stronger compliance evidence, lower risk, better decision quality, or measurable financial impact.

Adoption asks:

"Are people using AI?"

Implementation asks:

"Is AI making the business system better after cost, review, correction, exceptions, and risk are counted?"

This distinction changes how leaders manage AI.

A tool-first company celebrates when employees use the software.

A decision-first company asks whether AI improved the work that matters.

A tool-first company asks for more pilots.

A decision-first company asks which pilots deserve scale.

A tool-first company measures activity.

A decision-first company measures evidence.

Most organizations think the AI implementation problem is a software problem.

It is not.

It is a decision design problem.

The software may be powerful. The model may be impressive. The vendor may be credible. But if the organization does not define the workflow, the decision, the owner, the boundary, the risk, and the measurement method, the AI system floats inside the business without enough structure.

It may help.

It may confuse.

It may create value.

It may create hidden work.

Without implementation discipline, leaders cannot tell which is happening until the cost is already visible.

How AI Theater Usually Starts

AI Theater rarely begins with bad intent.

It usually begins with pressure.

The board asks about AI. Competitors announce AI initiatives. Employees start using AI informally. Vendors add AI features to every product. Executives read about automation. Customers expect faster service. Investors ask how the company plans to use AI.

Leadership responds by encouraging experimentation.

That is not wrong.

Experimentation is necessary. People closest to the work often discover useful opportunities first. A service desk technician knows which ticket notes waste time. A salesperson knows which account research steps are repetitive. A marketing manager knows which campaign planning tasks are slow. A finance analyst knows which reconciliations create repeated exceptions. A cybersecurity analyst knows which alert summaries are useful and which ones create false confidence.

Bottom-up experimentation can reveal practical friction that executives may never notice.

The problem begins when experimentation becomes the strategy.

A few early wins appear. Someone saves an hour drafting a report. Someone builds a useful prompt. Someone summarizes a security alert more clearly. Someone cleans up customer notes. Someone drafts a campaign faster.

Then stories turn into confidence.

Confidence turns into more pilots.

Pilots turn into dashboards.

Dashboards turn into "AI progress."

Then the harder questions arrive.

Which workflow improved?

Which decision became better?

Which cost went down?

Which risk went up?

Which employees are now reviewing more output than before?

Which AI results are being trusted without enough evidence?

Which pilots should scale?

Which should stop?

Which should be redesigned?

If the organization cannot answer those questions, it may have adoption, but it does not yet have implementation.

The theater is not the use of AI.

The theater is the absence of ownership, proof, and business discipline.

Bottom-Up Discovery, Top-Down Discipline

A serious AI implementation strategy should not crush bottom-up experimentation.

That would be a mistake.

Employees should be encouraged to notice friction, test ideas, and propose use cases. Many useful AI applications will come from the people closest to the workflow.

But bottom-up experimentation should create signals, not strategy.

A signal says:

"There may be value here."

Strategy asks:

"Should this be implemented, scaled, redesigned, or stopped?"

That second question requires leadership discipline.

Top-down implementation does not mean executives should micromanage prompts, tools, or every AI use case. That would be slow and unrealistic.

Top-down implementation means leadership defines the business priorities, decision rights, measurement standard, risk boundaries, and scale rules.

It means someone is responsible for deciding which AI experiments matter and which ones are noise.

Good top-down focus gives bottom-up experimentation a path. Employees can discover use cases. Managers can test them. The organization can measure them. Leaders can decide whether they deserve scale.

That is a healthy system.

The alternative is scattered experimentation with no center of gravity. Teams use different standards. Costs spread quietly. Data risks appear. The same problem is solved five different ways. Pilots compete for attention. Nobody knows what to stop.

In that environment, AI becomes an activity layer sitting on top of the business.

It does not become part of the operating system.

The Proof Gap

The Proof Gap is the space between an AI success story and a business case strong enough to justify scale.

Most AI pilots live inside this gap.

A team says AI saved time.

But how was the baseline measured?

Was the saved time real, or did it move to review?

Was correction time counted?

Were exceptions counted?

Did quality improve?

Did the customer experience improve?

Did risk increase?

Did the result depend on one skilled user?

Could ordinary users repeat the workflow safely?

What was the cost of the tool, integration, cloud usage, tokens, training, governance, monitoring, and oversight?

Did the output improve a business decision?

If those questions are not answered, the organization has a useful story, but not enough proof.

Stories matter. They help leaders notice opportunity.

But stories should not decide scale.

Evidence should.

The Proof Gap becomes dangerous when leaders treat early usefulness as implementation success. A pilot can be useful and still not deserve scale. A tool can save time for one employee and still fail economically across the business. A workflow can look faster and still increase risk.

The purpose of implementation discipline is not to kill useful AI experiments.

It is to protect the organization from scaling weak ones.

Adoption Metrics vs. Outcome Metrics

AI Theater survives because adoption metrics are easy to collect and easy to present.

The number of employees trained. The number of licenses assigned. The number of prompts submitted. The number of AI-generated documents. The number of meetings summarized. The number of support tickets classified. The number of departments using AI. The number of pilots launched.

These numbers are not useless.

They tell leaders whether AI activity exists.

But they do not prove business improvement.

A company can train 500 employees and still have no measurable value.

A team can generate 10,000 pieces of content and still weaken trust.

A service desk can summarize every ticket and still fail to reduce resolution time.

A finance team can classify invoices faster and still spend the same amount of time on exceptions.

A cybersecurity team can process more alerts and still fail to improve response quality.

Outcome metrics are different.

They measure whether the system improved.

For marketing and GTM, useful outcome metrics may include qualified pipeline, meeting conversion, sales acceptance, message quality, campaign-sourced opportunities, and trust with priority accounts.

For MSP and IT services, useful outcome metrics may include first-response time, resolution time, escalation accuracy, ticket reopen rate, technician review burden, client satisfaction, and cost per ticket.

For cybersecurity, useful outcome metrics may include time to triage, false-positive handling, escalation accuracy, analyst workload, response readiness, auditability, and incident response quality.

For finance, useful outcome metrics may include invoice exception rate, reconciliation time, approval accuracy, audit readiness, manual review burden, duplicate payment prevention, and cost per processed transaction.

Adoption metrics answer:

"Is AI being used?"

Outcome metrics answer:

"Is the business getting better?"

A serious AI implementation system uses both, but it never confuses them.

Adoption is the signal.

Outcome is the proof.

The AI Implementation Studio

To move from AI Theater to real implementation, organizations need a practical function that turns experiments into evidence and evidence into decisions.

That function is the AI Implementation Studio.

The AI Implementation Studio is not a software product.

It is not a vendor platform.

It is not a branding exercise.

It is an internal governance and execution function.

Its job is to select important workflows, require evidence, define decision boundaries, track total cost of ownership, measure rework, review risk, and decide what should scale, stop, or be redesigned.

The word "studio" is useful because a studio makes things. It does not only discuss policy. It shapes practical work. It tests ideas. It improves them. It rejects weak ones. It prepares strong ones for production.

A studio is not the same as a committee that meets once a month and produces documents nobody uses.

A good AI Implementation Studio is small enough to move, serious enough to say no, and practical enough to help teams improve real workflows.

In a large company, the Studio may include operations, IT, data, security, legal, finance, and business-unit leaders.

In a mid-market company, it may be a lean working group led by an operations leader, a technology leader, a finance-minded executive, and one or two workflow owners.

In a small business, it may be three people: the owner or general manager, the person closest to the workflow, and the person responsible for technology or risk.

The Studio does not need to be large. It does not need to be bureaucratic. It does not need a new department, a new title structure, or a formal innovation office.

It needs a clear function.

It exists to answer five practical questions:

What workflow is important enough to improve?

What decision inside that workflow should AI support?

What evidence proves the workflow improved?

What risks, costs, or rework are hidden?

Should this initiative scale, stop, or be redesigned?

That is the difference between AI Theater and implementation.

What the Studio Must Not Become

The AI Implementation Studio should not become another performance stage.

It should not collect shiny demos.

It should not approve every AI idea because "we need innovation."

It should not block every AI idea because "AI is risky."

It should not become a vendor showroom.

It should not produce long strategy decks instead of practical decisions.

It should not measure success by the number of pilots launched.

The Studio should be measured by the quality of the decisions it helps the organization make.

Did it identify the right workflows?

Did it prevent weak ideas from scaling?

Did it help strong use cases become safer and more measurable?

Did it expose hidden costs?

Did it define ownership?

Did it protect customer trust?

Did it improve the organization's ability to say yes, no, or not yet?

That last point is critical.

A serious AI implementation function must make it easier to say no.

Not because no is the goal.

Because yes becomes more valuable when it is earned.

The Evidence Pack

The main working document of the AI Implementation Studio is the Evidence Pack.

An Evidence Pack is a short, structured proof file for an AI use case. It should be practical enough for managers to complete and serious enough for executives to trust.

It is not a long consultant report.

It is not a marketing document.

It is not a vendor brochure.

It is a decision tool.

A good Evidence Pack should show what the organization knows before it decides whether to scale an AI initiative.

It should include the workflow, the decision being improved, the baseline, the AI-assisted process, the measured or estimated improvement, the review burden, the correction burden, the exception rate, the risk level, the human owner, the decision boundary, the total cost of ownership, and the recommendation.

The recommendation should be plain:

Scale. Stop. Redesign. Continue testing.

That is enough.

The Evidence Pack matters because it forces the organization to separate activity from proof.

A team may say, "AI saved us time."

The Evidence Pack asks, "How much time after review and correction?"

A team may say, "Employees like the tool."

The Evidence Pack asks, "Did the workflow improve?"

A team may say, "The pilot worked."

The Evidence Pack asks, "Can ordinary users repeat it safely?"

A team may say, "The vendor says this will scale."

The Evidence Pack asks, "What will it cost when usage increases?"

A team may say, "The output looks good."

The Evidence Pack asks, "Who owns the decision if it is wrong?"

That is why the Evidence Pack is not paperwork.

It is protection from self-deception.

In Practice: The Marketing Pilot That Looked Successful

The following is a modeled example for planning, not an audited client result.

A B2B marketing team launches an AI content pilot.

Before AI, the team produced eight pieces of campaign content per month.

After AI, the team produces twenty-four.

The first report says:

"AI increased marketing output by 200 percent."

That sounds impressive.

The AI Implementation Studio asks for an Evidence Pack.

The team reviews the actual business result.

Content volume increased. Website traffic improved slightly. Email open rates stayed flat. Reply rates declined. Sales complained that the messaging sounded generic. The brand lead found that many drafts needed heavy editing. The legal reviewer flagged unsupported claims. The CEO liked the speed but disliked the sameness.

The Evidence Pack shows that the pilot solved the wrong problem.

The bottleneck was not content production.

The bottleneck was message quality, proof, differentiation, and buyer relevance.

The Studio does not ban AI from marketing. AI can still help.

But the use case must change.

Instead of "generate more content," the new workflow becomes:

Use AI to turn approved buyer insights, proof points, customer objections, case notes, and product positioning into first-draft campaign briefs for specific segments.

That is a better implementation target.

It gives AI better inputs. It gives humans clearer review standards. It ties the workflow to buyer decisions. It reduces generic output. It protects trust.

The lesson is simple:

The first AI use case often reveals the real problem.

A weak organization celebrates the first version because it looks fast.

A stronger organization redesigns the use case so it creates value.

In Practice: The MSP Ticket Workflow

The following is a modeled example for planning, not an audited client result.

An MSP tests AI for ticket triage.

The first idea is broad:

"Use AI to classify and route support tickets."

That sounds useful, but it is too vague.

The AI Implementation Studio asks better questions.

Which ticket types? Which clients? Which risk levels? Which systems? Which user roles? What happens if the classification is wrong? Which tickets can AI route? Which tickets can AI only summarize? Which tickets must escalate? Which tickets should AI never downgrade?

The team runs a controlled test.

AI performs well on low-risk categories: password resets, basic access requests, simple software questions, printer issues, and routine how-to tickets.

It performs less reliably on tickets involving suspicious login behavior, backup failures, endpoint security alerts, executive users, network outages, and multi-user business interruption.

The Studio recommends a practical boundary.

AI may summarize most tickets. AI may recommend categories for low-risk and medium-risk tickets. AI may route only narrow low-risk ticket types. AI must escalate security-sensitive tickets. AI must stop when key context is missing.

The result is not full automation.

It is controlled implementation.

The MSP does not need AI to "take over" triage. It needs AI to reduce low-value work while protecting judgment in high-risk situations.

That is a serious use case.

Total Cost of Ownership

AI Theater usually focuses on the visible benefit and ignores the full cost.

A serious implementation must examine total cost of ownership.

For AI, total cost of ownership includes more than software licenses. It can include tool subscriptions, cloud usage, token costs, API costs, integration work, data preparation, security review, legal review, compliance work, workflow redesign, employee training, monitoring, human review, correction time, exception handling, governance time, vendor management, documentation, audit support, and ongoing maintenance.

Some costs are easy to see.

The vendor invoice is easy to see. The cost of human review is harder to see. The cloud bill is easy to see. The cost of exception handling is harder to see. The license price is easy to see. The cost of poor output quality is harder to see.

This is why total cost of ownership must be part of the Evidence Pack.

A workflow that looks profitable before review may not be profitable after review.

A tool that looks inexpensive in a pilot may become expensive at production volume.

A use case that looks safe in a controlled test may require stronger governance when connected to real customer data, financial systems, security tools, or regulated workflows.

The total-cost question is not meant to stop AI.

It is meant to prevent fake ROI.

The right question is not only:

"What does this cost now?"

The better question is:

"What does this cost if it works?"

That question prevents unpleasant surprises.

How to Move From Theater to Implementation

The move from AI Theater to real implementation does not require a giant transformation program.

It requires a disciplined sequence.

First, inventory what is already happening. Most organizations have more AI activity than leadership realizes. The goal is not to punish people for experimenting. The goal is to see reality.

Second, group AI activity by workflow. Do not organize the inventory only by tool. Tools change too quickly. Workflows are more stable: marketing campaign planning, sales prospect research, support ticket triage, invoice matching, security alert review, customer onboarding, proposal drafting, contract review, executive reporting.

Third, identify the decision inside each workflow. What decision is AI helping with? Is it helping decide what to send, what to approve, what to escalate, what to classify, what to investigate, what to prioritize, what to publish, what to ignore, or what to stop? If no decision can be named, the use case is probably too vague.

Fourth, assign an owner. Every AI use case needs a business owner, not just a tool user. Without ownership, AI activity becomes theater.

Fifth, define the boundary. Can AI assist, recommend, act, escalate, or stop? This should be clear before the organization scales the workflow.

Sixth, measure the baseline and the AI-assisted version. Count the visible gain and the hidden cost. Include verification, correction, exception handling, tool cost, token cost, cloud cost, integration, review, and governance.

Seventh, make a scale-or-stop decision. Scale if the evidence is strong. Stop if the value is weak or the risk is not justified. Redesign if the opportunity is real but the workflow, data, boundary, or measurement model is not ready.

This is how AI becomes a business implementation system instead of scattered activity.

Why Stopping Weak AI Projects Is a Strength

Many organizations struggle to stop AI projects because stopping feels like failure.

It is not.

Stopping a weak AI project is intelligent capital protection.

It means the organization learned something before wasting more money, time, trust, and management attention.

A project may need to stop because the workflow is unclear, the data is not ready, the risk is too high, the review burden erases the gain, the tool cost does not scale, the customer impact is weak, or the team is automating work that should be redesigned first.

This is not embarrassment.

It is discipline.

A mature organization does not ask:

"How many AI projects did we launch?"

It asks:

"Which AI projects earned the right to scale?"

That is a better standard.

The Real Goal

AI Theater says:

"Look how much we are doing."

Real implementation says:

"Look what changed, what it cost, who owns it, how we measured it, and why it deserves to continue."

That is the standard this book argues for.

The goal is not to make AI adoption slower. The goal is to make it more honest, more useful, and more scalable.

A company should experiment. It should learn. It should let employees discover practical uses. It should test new tools. It should remain curious.

But it should not confuse curiosity with implementation.

Implementation begins when AI is connected to a workflow, a decision, an owner, a boundary, a cost model, and a measurable outcome.

That is when the organization moves from AI Theater to AI discipline.

And that is when AI starts to become more than activity.

It becomes part of how the business improves.

Decision Architect's Field Notes

What to Do Next

Choose three AI activities already happening in your organization.

For each one, answer five questions:

What workflow does this activity support?

What decision does it help improve?

Who owns the outcome?

What metric proves the workflow improved?

What hidden cost or risk could erase the benefit?

If you cannot answer these questions, the activity may still be useful, but it is not yet ready to scale.

Next, create a simple Evidence Pack for one AI use case. Keep it short. One or two pages is enough.

Include the workflow, baseline, AI-assisted process, review burden, correction burden, exception rate, total cost of ownership, decision boundary, risk level, owner, and recommendation.

The recommendation should be one of four choices:

Scale. Stop. Redesign. Continue testing.

The goal is not paperwork.

The goal is better decisions.

Common Traps to Avoid

Do not treat employee AI usage as proof of implementation.

Do not count pilots as business outcomes.

Do not scale an AI use case because the demo looked impressive.

Do not measure output volume without measuring quality, review, correction, and exceptions.

Do not ignore tool, cloud, token, integration, review, and governance costs.

Do not use governance as an excuse to freeze useful experimentation.

Do not use experimentation as an excuse to avoid ownership.

Do not automate a workflow until the decision boundary is clear.

Boardroom Question

Which AI activities in our organization have enough evidence, ownership, cost clarity, and decision boundaries to justify scale — and which ones are still theater?

Industry Translation

In marketing and GTM, AI Theater appears when teams produce more content, more campaigns, and more outreach without improving buyer trust, qualified pipeline, sales acceptance, or conversion quality.

In MSP and IT services, it appears when AI summarizes and routes tickets faster, but senior technicians still carry the real judgment burden and escalation rules remain unclear.

In cybersecurity, it appears when AI accelerates alert summaries but does not improve triage quality, escalation accuracy, response readiness, or analyst trust.

In finance, it appears when AI speeds up document handling or invoice matching, but exceptions, approvals, audit trails, and high-risk payments still require the same or greater human review.

Across all these systems, the pattern is the same:

Activity looks like progress until ownership, cost, risk, and outcomes are measured.

Implementation Law

Activity without ownership is theater.

Chapter 3 - The Rework Tax: The Silent Killer of Scaling

Why Hidden Correction, Verification, Exception Handling, and Review Costs Determine Whether AI Scales

The pilot looked profitable.

On the first dashboard, the story was clean. A support workflow that used to take twelve minutes now took four. A marketing brief that used to take two hours now took twenty minutes. A finance review that used to require manual extraction now had most fields filled in by AI. A cybersecurity analyst who used to read long alert histories now received a polished summary in seconds.

The team was ready to celebrate.

Then the operations leader asked to see the full workflow.

The support team still checked whether the AI summary missed customer history. The marketing manager still rewrote generic language and removed unsupported claims. The finance analyst still investigated exceptions because the easy invoices were never the real problem. The cybersecurity analyst still verified asset criticality, user privilege, related alerts, and containment risk before trusting the summary.

The AI output was fast.

The trusted output was not nearly as fast.

That difference is the Rework Tax.

The Rework Tax is the hidden time spent verifying, correcting, reviewing, and managing AI output before it can be trusted inside a real business process. The word "tax" is used here as a metaphor. It is not a legal or government tax. It is the operational cost that appears after the impressive first output.

This is one of the main reasons AI pilots look better than AI implementations.

A pilot often measures how fast AI creates something.

A real implementation must measure how much work remains before that something can be used safely, confidently, and economically.

That is where many AI business cases become weaker.

Not because AI is useless.

Because the math was incomplete.

The blind spot is this:

Organizations measure AI's first output, not trusted usable output.

They measure generation, not verification. They measure speed, not correction. They measure output, not exception handling. They measure adoption, not trust.

This creates a distorted picture of productivity.

A company may believe a task became 70 percent faster because AI produced a first version quickly. But if humans must spend meaningful time checking, fixing, rerouting, explaining, documenting, or cleaning up that output, the real gain may be much smaller.

In some workflows, the gain may disappear.

In high-risk workflows, the AI-assisted process may become more expensive than the original process because it adds review without removing enough work.

That does not mean AI failed.

It means the organization measured the wrong layer.

AI can create value. But value does not appear at the moment of output. Value appears when the output becomes trusted enough to move the business process forward.

That is why the Rework Tax matters.

It separates AI activity from AI economics.

The Formula That Prevents Fake Productivity Math

The simplest way to measure the Rework Tax is through the Net Gain formula:

Net Gain = (Baseline Time − AI-Assisted Time) − (Verification + Correction + Exception Handling)

This formula is not meant to be perfect accounting.

It is meant to prevent fake productivity math.

Baseline Time is how long the work took before AI.

AI-Assisted Time is how long the AI-assisted first version takes.

Verification is the time spent checking whether the output is accurate, complete, relevant, safe, and usable.

Correction is the time spent fixing the output.

Exception Handling is the time spent dealing with cases where AI cannot complete the work, creates uncertainty, misses context, or sends the work back to humans.

The formula asks one practical question:

After the human cleanup work is counted, is there still a meaningful gain?

That question should appear in every serious AI pilot review.

Without it, the organization may present gross speed as net value.

Gross speed is not enough.

A workflow is not better because the first draft appears faster. It is better only if the completed, trusted, usable work improves after all necessary review and correction are counted.

A Modeled Example: The Report That Almost Fooled the Team

The following is a modeled example for planning purposes, not an audited client result.

A mid-sized professional services firm tests AI for weekly client performance reports.

Before AI, each report takes 90 minutes.

With AI, the first draft takes 20 minutes.

The team's first claim is simple:

"AI saves 70 minutes per report."

That sounds strong. If the company produces 200 reports per month, the apparent savings is 14,000 minutes, or more than 230 hours.

Then the manager measures the full workflow.

The AI draft is fast, but the trusted report still requires work:

Baseline Time: 90 minutes
AI-Assisted First Draft: 20 minutes
Verification: 18 minutes
Correction: 14 minutes
Exception Handling: 9 minutes

Now the calculation changes:

Net Gain = (90 − 20) − (18 + 14 + 9)

Net Gain = 70 − 41

Net Gain = 29 minutes

The workflow still improved.

But it did not improve by 70 minutes.

It improved by 29 minutes.

That is still useful. Across 200 reports per month, 29 minutes per report could create real capacity. But the business case is now honest.

The first version said:

"AI reduced report time by 78 percent."

The corrected version says:

"AI created a 29-minute net gain per report after verification, correction, and exception handling."

The second sentence is less exciting.

It is also more useful.

Now leadership can decide intelligently. Maybe the workflow deserves scale. Maybe it needs better data inputs. Maybe the review standard should be improved. Maybe AI should generate only the report structure and draft commentary, while humans own recommendations. Maybe the process should require source links for every claim.

The formula does not kill the project.

It improves the decision.

That is the point.

When the Rework Tax Erases the Gain

Some AI workflows still produce strong net gain after rework is counted.

Others do not.

The Rework Tax becomes dangerous when it quietly consumes the value.

Before AI, a finance analyst spends 10 minutes reviewing a routine invoice.

With AI, the invoice is pre-classified in two minutes.

The apparent savings is eight minutes.

But the analyst spends four minutes verifying vendor details, two minutes checking purchase order alignment, and three minutes handling exception flags because the AI is uncertain.

The calculation becomes:

Net Gain = (10 − 2) − (4 + 2 + 3)

Net Gain = 8 − 9

Net Gain = -1 minute

The AI-assisted workflow is one minute slower.

This does not mean AI should be abandoned in finance. It means this workflow, at this level of reliability, data quality, boundary design, and exception handling, does not yet justify scale.

The correct response is not emotional.

It is operational.

Narrow the use case. Improve the inputs. Separate routine cases from exceptions. Change the AI role from "classify" to "prepare for review." Add clearer escalation rules. Or stop the project and move resources to a stronger use case.

The worst response is to scale anyway because the demo looked good.

Real Velocity: The Cost That Arrives Later

Net Gain is useful for managers, consultants, and business operators because it is simple.

For operations, engineering, cybersecurity, and systems-oriented readers, a second concept is useful:

Real Velocity = AI Output Speed − (Detection Latency + Rework Time)

AI Output Speed is how quickly AI creates an output.

Detection Latency is the time it takes for humans or systems to notice that something is wrong, incomplete, risky, unclear, or misrouted.

Rework Time is the time required to fix the issue.

This matters because not every AI error is detected immediately.

Some mistakes are obvious. A wrong customer name can be seen. A broken calculation can be checked. A strange tone in a customer email may be caught during review.

Other errors hide.

A weak cybersecurity classification may not be noticed until the incident grows. A poor sales message may not be noticed until response rates decline. A bad finance classification may not be noticed until audit cleanup. A misleading support summary may not be noticed until the customer complains. A flawed code suggestion may not be noticed until maintenance becomes harder.

AI speed can be deceptive because the output arrives now and the cost arrives later.

Real Velocity forces the organization to ask:

How fast are we really moving after delayed detection and correction are counted?

A slower workflow with low rework may outperform a faster workflow with hidden cleanup.

That is not anti-AI.

That is implementation reality.

Why Unit Economics Collapse at Scale

The Rework Tax becomes most dangerous when the organization scales.

In a small pilot, hidden review work can be absorbed by motivated users. A senior manager checks the output. A technical expert supervises the workflow. A project champion fixes mistakes quietly. A vendor engineer helps with setup. Everyone is paying attention because the pilot is visible.

The economics look better because the support structure is informal.

Production is different.

Production includes ordinary users, higher volume, messier data, edge cases, staff turnover, deadlines, customer pressure, audit needs, security requirements, integration costs, and less patience.

A workflow that works for one expert may fail when twenty employees use it. A workflow that works on 100 clean examples may struggle with 10,000 messy cases. A workflow that works in one department may create review burden in another. A workflow that works during a pilot may become expensive when tool usage, cloud cost, token consumption, monitoring, governance, and exception handling increase.

This is how unit economics collapse.

The cost per completed unit does not fall as expected.

It may rise.

The company thought AI would reduce labor per transaction, per ticket, per report, per invoice, per alert, or per campaign.

Instead, AI creates a new layer of review and exception management.

The organization gets more output but not enough completed work.

This is the scaling problem.

AI does not scale because the first output is fast.

AI scales when the cost of producing trusted usable output falls.

That distinction is brutal but necessary.

The Gartner Warning, Used Carefully

Gartner predicted in June 2025 that more than 40 percent of agentic AI projects would be canceled by the end of 2027 because of escalating costs, unclear business value, or inadequate risk controls. Gartner also described many current agentic AI projects as early-stage experiments or proofs of concept, often driven by hype or misapplied use cases.

This prediction should be used carefully.

It does not mean AI is failing.

It does not mean agentic AI has no future.

It does not mean the Rework Tax alone explains the entire cancellation pattern.

The warning is broader. It points to the gap between AI possibility and operational reality.

Escalating cost, unclear business value, and inadequate risk controls are exactly the conditions that appear when organizations scale AI without understanding the real workflow economics.

The Rework Tax is one mechanism inside that broader problem.

Integration cost is another. Poor data is another. Weak boundaries are another. Vendor overstatement is another. Unclear ownership is another. Risk exposure is another.

The point is not to use the Gartner prediction as fear marketing.

The point is to use it as a discipline reminder.

AI projects do not deserve scale because they are impressive.

They deserve scale when they have evidence.

Review Cost Is Often the Most Expensive Cost

Human review is easy to underestimate because it does not always look like work.

A manager "just checks" the AI draft.

A senior technician "just looks over" the ticket summary.

A finance analyst "just confirms" the fields.

A security analyst "just verifies" the alert context.

A lawyer "just reviews" the generated language.

Those words hide cost.

Just checking still takes time. Just verifying still uses expert attention. Just correcting still delays the workflow. Just approving still carries accountability.

In many organizations, the most expensive people become the invisible review layer for AI output.

That matters.

If AI saves junior staff time but consumes senior expert time, the economics may be weaker than the dashboard suggests.

This is especially important in MSPs, cybersecurity, finance, healthcare administration, legal review, and executive decision support. In those environments, expert attention is scarce. Using it poorly can be more expensive than the original manual process.

The question is not:

"Did AI reduce somebody's time?"

The better question is:

"Did AI reduce the right time without increasing higher-cost review work?"

That question changes the conversation.

Exception Handling: Where the Hard Cost Lives

AI pilots often focus on average performance.

Averages can hide exceptions.

A workflow may perform well 80 percent of the time and become expensive in the remaining 20 percent. That remaining 20 percent may determine whether the use case scales.

In finance, exceptions may involve changed bank details, mismatched invoices, new vendors, missing purchase orders, unusually high amounts, duplicate payment signals, or rushed payment requests.

In cybersecurity, exceptions may involve privileged users, sensitive systems, repeated alerts, suspicious geography, unusual access patterns, unclear asset criticality, or ambiguous containment risk.

In MSP support, exceptions may involve executive users, outages, security-sensitive tickets, VIP clients, unclear client context, or contractual response obligations.

In marketing, exceptions may involve regulated claims, unsupported customer results, competitive comparisons, industry-specific wording, or content that could damage trust.

Exceptions matter because they often carry disproportionate risk.

The routine cases may be easy.

The exceptions are where the business gets hurt.

A serious AI implementation must ask:

What percentage of cases are exceptions?
How expensive are those exceptions?
Who handles them?
How quickly are they detected?
What is the escalation path?
Can the workflow separate routine cases from risky cases early?

This is where Decision Architecture becomes practical.

AI does not need to handle every case.

It needs to know when not to pretend.

Short Industry Translation: MSP Ticket Triage

Consider an MSP that uses AI to summarize and classify support tickets.

Before AI, a Level 1 technician spends six minutes reading a ticket and assigning a category.

With AI, the summary and suggested category appear in one minute.

The apparent savings is five minutes per ticket.

At 2,000 tickets per month, the first estimate looks excellent.

But then the service manager measures review.

Low-risk tickets work well. Password resets, simple software questions, routine access requests, and basic how-to tickets show clear improvement.

But security-sensitive tickets, executive-user issues, backup failures, endpoint alerts, and multi-user outages still require senior review.

Now the economics are different.

The MSP may be saving Level 1 time while consuming senior technician time.

That is not automatically a bad trade. But it must be measured honestly.

The redesign is not to abandon AI.

The redesign is to narrow the boundary.

AI can summarize most tickets. AI can recommend classification for low-risk tickets. AI can route only pre-approved categories with clear signals. AI must escalate security-sensitive, executive, outage, backup, identity, or multi-user issues. AI must stop when client context is missing.

Now the Rework Tax becomes manageable because the workflow separates routine work from judgment-heavy work.

That is how AI starts to scale.

Not by pretending every ticket is the same.

By designing the boundary around the real cost of being wrong.

The Rework Tax Is a Design Signal

The Rework Tax is not only a cost.

It is a diagnostic signal.

High verification time may mean the AI output lacks sources, traceability, or required evidence.

High correction time may mean prompts, data inputs, templates, or workflow rules are weak.

High exception handling may mean the use case is too broad.

High senior review time may mean the workflow touches riskier decisions than leaders realized.

High user frustration may mean AI was inserted into the wrong step.

High downstream cleanup may mean the organization measured the wrong output.

A weak organization treats the Rework Tax as employee resistance.

A strong organization treats it as workflow intelligence.

If employees keep correcting AI output, ask why.

If managers do not trust the results, ask what evidence is missing.

If experts must review everything, ask whether the decision boundary is too broad.

If exceptions are common, ask whether the workflow should be split into routine and high-risk paths.

The Rework Tax is not just a financial number.

It is a map of where AI does not yet fit.

The Scale Decision

At the end of an AI pilot, the organization should not ask only:

"Did it work?"

That question is too vague.

A better scale decision asks:

Did it create a net gain after verification, correction, and exception handling?

Did it reduce the right kind of work?

Did it increase senior review burden?

Did it improve decision quality?

Did it reduce risk or increase it?

Did it hold up across ordinary users, not only power users?

Did the total cost of ownership still make sense?

Did the workflow become easier to manage?

Did the evidence justify scale?

These questions turn AI from a pilot story into a business decision.

The answer may be scale.

The answer may be redesign.

The answer may be stop.

All three are valid.

The only invalid answer is scaling without understanding the real cost.

The Real Lesson

AI speed is only the beginning.

The real question is what happens after the output appears.

Who checks it?

Who corrects it?

Who trusts it?

Who owns it?

Who handles exceptions?

Who pays for the review?

Who is accountable if it is wrong?

Can the workflow still produce value after those costs are counted?

That is the discipline many AI adoption efforts avoid.

It is also the discipline that determines whether AI scales.

When the Rework Tax is low and the business value is high, scale may make sense.

When the Rework Tax is high but the risk reduction or expert leverage is valuable, redesign may make sense.

When the Rework Tax erases the gain and the workflow does not improve, stopping may be the best decision.

That is mature AI implementation.

Not more hype.

Not more pilots.

Not more output.

A clear understanding of whether AI makes the business system better after the hidden work is counted.

Decision Architect's Field Notes

What to Do Next

Choose one active AI workflow and measure the full work, not just the first AI output.

Take a small sample of real cases. Twenty-five cases are enough to begin. For each case, record the baseline time, AI-assisted time, verification time, correction time, exception handling time, reviewer role, risk level, and final outcome.

Then calculate:

Net Gain = (Baseline Time − AI-Assisted Time) − (Verification + Correction + Exception Handling)

Do not argue about perfect measurement at the beginning. Start with practical measurement. The first sample will usually reveal the pattern.

Then ask whether the gain is large enough to justify scale.

Common Traps to Avoid

Do not claim AI saved time before verification, correction, and exception handling are counted.

Do not assume the first draft is the finished work.

Do not ignore senior review time.

Do not average routine cases and high-risk exceptions together.

Do not scale a workflow that only works when a power user supervises it.

Do not treat correction work as employee resistance. It may be evidence that the implementation design is weak.

Do not present gross savings as ROI.

Do not forget that a small error rate can become expensive at high volume.

Boardroom Question

After we count verification, correction, exception handling, senior review, delayed error detection, and total cost of ownership, which AI workflows still create a defensible net gain?

Industry Translation

In MSP and IT services, the Rework Tax appears when AI speeds up ticket summaries but senior technicians still review classifications, escalations, client context, and security-sensitive signals.

In finance, it appears when AI processes routine invoices quickly but exceptions, high-value approvals, changed payment details, and audit trails still require careful human review.

In cybersecurity, it appears when AI summarizes alerts quickly but analysts still verify severity, asset criticality, user privilege, response actions, and containment risk.

In marketing and GTM, it appears when AI multiplies content but managers, sales teams, legal reviewers, and brand leaders spend more time fixing generic, unsupported, or trust-damaging output.

Implementation Law

AI does not scale on output speed. It scales on trusted net gain.

Chapter 4 - The Pilot Trap and the 40% Failure Pattern

Why Successful AI Pilots Still Fail at Scale

The pilot was a success.

That was the official summary.

The demo worked. The users liked it. The vendor was responsive. The internal champion was respected. The output looked better than expected. A few early users said it saved time. The executive sponsor saw enough to approve the next step.

The project moved from "interesting experiment" to "strategic initiative."

Then production began.

The clean pilot data became messy operating data. The five trained pilot users became fifty ordinary users. The workflow touched systems nobody had connected during the test. Legal asked for audit trails. Security asked where data was going. Finance asked why usage costs were rising. Operations asked who owned exceptions. Customer support asked what to do when the AI was uncertain. Managers asked why the process worked well for the original team but not for everyone else.

The pilot had proved possibility.

It had not proved production readiness.

That is the Pilot Trap.

The Pilot Trap happens when an organization treats a successful AI pilot as evidence that the system is ready to scale.

Sometimes it is.

Often it is not.

The blind spot is simple:

Pilot success is not production readiness.

A pilot can be useful, impressive, and worth learning from — and still not be ready for expansion. A pilot can show that AI can help one workflow under controlled conditions. It does not automatically show that the workflow can survive real volume, messy data, ordinary users, integration requirements, risk controls, cost pressure, customer exposure, and executive accountability.

This distinction matters because AI pilots are often designed to succeed.

Production is not.

Production is designed to reveal what the pilot avoided.

Why Pilots Are Designed to Succeed

Most pilots are built inside favorable conditions.

The use case is narrowed. The data sample is cleaned. The users are motivated. The project team is attentive. The vendor is engaged. The workflow is watched closely. Exceptions are handled manually. Senior people quietly step in when something becomes unclear.

That does not make the pilot dishonest.

It makes it incomplete.

A pilot is supposed to test possibility. It asks, "Could AI help here?"

That is a legitimate question.

But it is not the final question.

A pilot environment often hides the conditions that determine whether AI can actually scale. It may not include full integration cost. It may not include ordinary user behavior. It may not include edge cases. It may not include compliance review. It may not include production monitoring. It may not include data drift. It may not include all exception paths. It may not include downstream impact on other teams.

It may also depend heavily on one skilled user.

This is common. One employee learns the tool deeply, writes better prompts, understands the workflow, fixes mistakes, and becomes the unofficial interpreter between AI and the business. The pilot looks strong because the power user is strong.

Then the project scales.

Ordinary users do not use the tool the same way. They do not know what to check. They do not see subtle errors. They trust too much or distrust everything. They do not understand the boundary. They do not know which outputs require escalation.

The pilot did not test the system.

It tested the system plus a gifted babysitter.

That is not a scalable operating model.

Why Production Is Different

Production is where the business stops admiring AI and starts depending on it.

That changes everything.

In production, the workflow must handle volume. It must survive ordinary usage. It must work with real data, not just clean examples. It must integrate with business systems. It must produce evidence. It must support auditability. It must define who owns decisions. It must handle failures. It must manage exceptions. It must control cost. It must protect customer trust.

Production also introduces a different emotional environment.

During the pilot, people are curious.

During production, people are accountable.

A manager may enjoy testing AI on a small group of internal documents. That same manager will behave differently when the AI output affects customers, invoices, compliance, cybersecurity response, healthcare administration, legal language, or executive reporting.

The risk threshold rises.

The tolerance for ambiguity falls.

The need for documentation increases.

The cost of being wrong becomes more concrete.

This is why the move from pilot to production cannot be treated as a larger version of the pilot. It is a different stage of implementation.

The pilot asks:

Can this work?

Production asks:

Can this work repeatedly, safely, economically, and with clear ownership inside the real business system?

Those are not the same question.

The Gartner Warning, Used Without Fear Marketing

The gap between a pilot and production is where most AI initiatives quietly die. In 2025, this became mathematically undeniable.

Research from MIT revealed that 95 percent of enterprise generative AI pilots failed to deliver measurable financial ROI. Furthermore, IDC reported that 88 percent of AI projects never left the pilot phase at all. They became stuck in pilot purgatory - impressive in the demo, but completely unable to survive the messy reality of integration, risk controls, and ordinary users.

This is not a technology failure.

It is a symptom of the Pilot Trap. The organization built for the demo. It did not build for the business system.

This should not be used as fear marketing.

It does not mean AI is failing.

It does not mean agentic AI has no business future.

It does not mean every AI pilot is doomed.

It means many organizations are discovering the difference between AI possibility and production reality.

That is the useful lesson.

The 40 percent warning fits the pattern this chapter addresses: projects that look promising in controlled settings can stall when they face cost, risk, governance, integration, data quality, and business-value tests. The failure pattern is not usually one dramatic collapse. It is often a slow loss of confidence.

Costs rise.

Value remains vague.

Risk controls lag behind enthusiasm.

The pilot still looks good in memory, but the production case becomes harder to defend.

A serious organization does not respond by avoiding AI.

It responds by building better stage gates.

Productionization Cost

Productionization cost is the cost of turning an AI pilot into a reliable operating capability.

This cost is often underestimated.

It can include workflow redesign, data preparation, system integration, access control, security review, legal review, compliance mapping, user training, monitoring, logging, escalation rules, vendor management, cloud usage, token usage, documentation, audit support, exception handling, and ongoing maintenance.

The pilot may only show the feature.

Production reveals the system.

This is especially important with agentic AI, where the tool may not only generate output but also take steps, call tools, retrieve information, trigger workflows, recommend actions, or operate across systems. The more the AI can do, the more important productionization becomes.

A narrow assistant that drafts internal notes may need limited controls.

An AI workflow that touches customer communication, security alerts, financial approvals, employee records, medical administration, legal language, or operational decisions needs far stronger controls.

The cost is not only technical.

It is organizational.

Who owns the workflow?

Who approves the decision boundary?

Who monitors performance?

Who handles exceptions?

Who decides when the AI must stop?

Who explains the outcome if a customer, auditor, regulator, executive, or board member asks?

If those questions are unanswered, the pilot is not ready for production.

It may still be promising.

But promise is not readiness.

Stage Gates: How Pilots Earn the Right to Scale

A practical AI implementation system needs stage gates.

A stage gate is a decision checkpoint. It forces the organization to decide whether a project should continue, scale, stop, or be redesigned before more money and trust are committed.

Stage gates are not bureaucracy when used properly.

They are protection against self-deception.

A useful AI pilot should pass through six gates.

Workflow Fit

Decision Fit

Evidence and Economics Fit

Boundary Fit

Risk Fit

Production Fit

Gate 1: Workflow Fit

The organization must define the workflow clearly.

Not "use AI in finance" or "use AI in support." That is too broad. The workflow must be specific enough to measure.

For example: classify low-risk support tickets, draft first-response messages for approved categories, extract invoice fields for routine vendors, summarize security alerts for analyst review, or generate campaign briefs from approved positioning inputs.

If the workflow cannot be named clearly, the pilot is not ready.

Gate 2: Decision Fit

The organization must identify the decision AI supports.

Does AI help decide what to classify, what to route, what to escalate, what to approve, what to draft, what to investigate, what to ignore, or what to recommend?

If no decision can be named, the project is likely too vague.

AI should not be implemented as decoration. It should support a real decision or workflow step.

Gate 3: Evidence and Economics Fit

The organization must compare the baseline and the AI-assisted workflow.

This includes time, quality, review burden, correction burden, exception rate, user experience, customer impact, and total cost.

This gate connects directly to the Evidence Pack introduced earlier. The point is not to create paperwork. The point is to force a clean decision.

What changed?

How do we know?

What did it cost?

What improved after review, correction, exception handling, and tool usage were counted?

A pilot that saves time but increases senior review burden may not be economically strong. A pilot that works only because a power user supervises it may not be scalable. A pilot that looks cheap in a small test may become expensive when usage, cloud cost, token cost, monitoring, and support increase.

This gate prevents the organization from mistaking gross improvement for net value.

Gate 4: Boundary Fit

The organization must define what AI can do alone, what it can recommend, what must be reviewed, and what must remain human-owned.

This is where many pilots fail quietly.

They prove that AI can assist but then pretend it can act. They prove that AI can summarize but then let people treat the summary as a decision. They prove that AI can recommend but fail to define who owns the recommendation.

Without a boundary, production becomes dangerous.

Gate 5: Risk Fit

The organization must decide whether the risk level matches the AI role.

A low-risk internal draft may only need light review. A customer-facing response needs stronger controls. A finance approval, cybersecurity escalation, healthcare administrative message, legal summary, or compliance-sensitive workflow needs much tighter ownership, evidence, and auditability.

Risk Fit asks:

What happens if AI is wrong?

Who is affected?

Can the error be detected quickly?

Can it be corrected safely?

Does the workflow involve money, security, customer trust, regulated data, legal exposure, patient information, or operational continuity?

If the risk is high, AI may still be useful. But its role must be narrower. It may assist, summarize, organize evidence, or recommend. It should not silently act beyond the boundary.

This gate protects the business from scaling confidence faster than accountability.

Gate 6: Production Fit

The organization must decide whether the workflow can survive real operating conditions.

This includes ordinary users, real data, expected volume, integration needs, monitoring, training, escalation, compliance, security, vendor reliability, cost behavior, ownership, and support burden.

This is the gate many pilots skip.

It is also the gate that determines whether the project deserves scale.

A project can pass Workflow Fit, Decision Fit, and Evidence and Economics Fit, but still fail Production Fit. That is not failure. That is learning before damage.

Production Fit asks the final question:

Can this AI workflow work repeatedly, safely, economically, and with clear ownership inside the real business system?

If the answer is yes, scale may be justified.

If the answer is no, the right decision is redesign, continue testing with a specific question, or stop.

Scale-or-Stop Discipline

Scale-or-stop discipline is the practice of deciding before and after a pilot whether an AI initiative deserves expansion, redesign, or termination.

The phrase matters because many organizations have a hidden third category: endless continuation.

The pilot does not fail.

It does not scale.

It just keeps consuming attention.

A few people keep using it. A few meetings keep referencing it. The vendor relationship continues. The tool remains in the stack. Nobody wants to declare it weak because it once looked promising.

This is how AI clutter accumulates.

A serious organization does not let pilots drift.

It makes one of four decisions:

Scale.

Redesign.

Continue testing with a specific unanswered question.

Stop.

The third option must be used carefully. "Continue testing" should not mean "avoid making a decision." It should mean the project has one or two specific unknowns that can be answered within a defined period.

For example:

Can ordinary users achieve similar results?

Can the exception rate be reduced?

Can the workflow run safely with real data?

Can integration cost stay within the business case?

Can the AI output meet the required trust threshold?

If the next test does not answer a specific question, it is not a test.

It is delay.

Stopping a weak project is not failure. It is intelligent capital protection.

It protects time, money, trust, attention, and credibility. It also protects stronger AI projects from being crowded out by weaker ones.

The ability to stop is what makes scaling more trustworthy.

When every project gets approved, approval means very little.

When projects must earn scale, scale becomes a serious decision.

A Modeled Example: The Support Pilot That Passed the Demo and Failed the Desk

The following is a modeled example for planning purposes, not an audited client result.

A mid-sized B2B service company tests AI for customer support ticket triage.

The pilot goal is simple: reduce the time required to summarize, classify, and route incoming tickets.

The pilot uses 200 historical tickets. The data is fairly clean. A support manager selects examples across common categories. Three experienced agents participate. The AI summarizes the issue, suggests a category, recommends priority, and drafts an internal note.

The pilot results look strong.

Average triage time drops from seven minutes to three minutes.

Agents like the summaries.

The manager estimates four minutes saved per ticket.

With 5,000 tickets per month, the projected savings look meaningful.

Leadership approves production expansion.

Then the workflow reaches the real service desk.

The first problem is user variation. The pilot agents were experienced. Newer agents do not always know when the AI summary is incomplete.

The second problem is ticket quality. Live tickets are messier than historical examples. Customers include screenshots without explanation. Some tickets include outdated subject lines. Some issues combine billing, access, technical support, and security concerns in one thread.

The third problem is escalation. The AI performs well on routine requests but struggles with tickets involving VIP accounts, business outages, suspicious login behavior, contract-specific service levels, and unclear client context.

The fourth problem is integration. The AI summary does not always map cleanly into the ticketing system's fields. Agents copy and paste. Managers later ask why reports do not match actual categories.

The fifth problem is cost. Usage increases faster than expected because agents begin using AI multiple times per ticket: once for summary, once for reply draft, once for classification, and once for escalation notes.

The pilot was not fake.

It was incomplete.

The AI clearly helped with routine triage. But the production workflow exposed missing boundaries, weak exception handling, unclear escalation rules, integration friction, and underestimated usage cost.

A weak organization would blame the tool or blame the users.

A stronger organization would redesign the implementation.

The revised plan is narrower.

AI may summarize all tickets, but the summary must show missing information. AI may recommend categories for routine tickets, but it may not auto-route tickets involving security language, executive users, outages, payment issues, or contract-sensitive accounts. AI must flag uncertain classifications. Agents receive a short review standard. The ticketing fields are redesigned so AI output maps into structured categories instead of free-text notes. Usage is monitored by workflow step, not just total volume.

The decision changes from "scale the pilot" to "scale the safe portion of the workflow."

That is the lesson.

The pilot proved possibility.

Production revealed the real design.

The Red Flag: "It Worked in the Pilot"

One of the most dangerous sentences in AI implementation is:

"It worked in the pilot."

That sentence is not wrong.

It is incomplete.

A pilot result should start a production-readiness conversation, not end it.

When someone says the pilot worked, leaders should ask:

Under what conditions?

With which users?

On what data?

With what review burden?

At what cost?

With what exception rate?

With what risk boundary?

With what integration requirement?

With what monitoring?

With what owner?

With what failure path?

Those questions do not weaken the pilot.

They make the pilot useful.

A pilot that cannot answer those questions may still be valuable as discovery. It may show that the opportunity is real. It may reveal where the workflow is broken. It may show that AI should assist rather than act. It may expose a data problem the organization needed to solve anyway.

But it should not be treated as proof of production value.

A successful pilot proves possibility.

Production proves value.

Decision Architect's Field Notes

What to Do Next

Choose one AI pilot that your organization considers successful.

Do not review the demo. Review the production path.

Ask five questions:

What workflow did the pilot actually test?

What decision did AI support?

What conditions made the pilot easier than production?

What costs appear only when the workflow scales?

What must be true before this deserves expansion?

Then assign the pilot one of four decisions: scale, redesign, continue testing with a specific unanswered question, or stop.

Do not allow "keep exploring" as a vague answer. Exploration is useful only when it is attached to a clear question.

Common Traps to Avoid

Do not treat pilot enthusiasm as production evidence.

Do not assume power-user success means ordinary-user readiness.

Do not scale from clean data to messy data without a production test.

Do not ignore integration, monitoring, training, security, audit, and exception-handling costs.

Do not let a pilot continue forever because nobody wants to stop it.

Do not call something scalable until the workflow has an owner, a boundary, a cost model, and a failure path.

Boardroom Question

Which AI pilots have actually earned the right to scale, and which ones are only successful under controlled conditions?

Industry Translation

In MSP and IT services, the Pilot Trap appears when AI handles clean ticket samples but struggles with live client context, escalation rules, VIP users, outages, and security-sensitive issues.

In finance, it appears when AI performs well on routine documents but fails to justify automation for exception-heavy approvals, payment risk, audit evidence, or unusual transactions.

In cybersecurity, it appears when AI summarizes alerts well in testing but cannot safely influence response decisions without asset context, severity ownership, and escalation rules.

In marketing and GTM, it appears when AI produces strong sample campaigns but fails at scale because the output becomes generic, unsupported, or disconnected from buyer trust.

Implementation Law

A successful pilot proves possibility. Production proves value.

Chapter 5 - Trust, Risk, and the Shadow Ledger

Why Ownership Matters More Than Confidence

The finance team did not think AI had approved the payment.

Technically, it had not.

The AI system had summarized the vendor record, checked the invoice fields, compared the purchase order, and marked the transaction as routine. The analyst saw the summary. The manager saw the green status. The payment moved forward.

Two weeks later, the CFO asked why an unusual vendor change had not been escalated.

The answer came back in fragments.

The analyst said the AI summary did not highlight the issue. The manager said the analyst had approved the queue. The finance operations lead said the system was only advisory. IT said the tool had no authority to approve payments. The vendor said the workflow was configured according to customer preference. Compliance asked where the review record was. Nobody could show exactly who had owned the risk decision.

Everyone had touched the process.

No one clearly owned the outcome.

That is the trust problem.

In business systems, AI does not need formal approval authority to influence a decision. It can influence a decision by summarizing information, ranking options, labeling risk, drafting recommendations, hiding uncertainty, or making one path look easier than another.

The organization may say, "AI did not decide."

But if people acted because of what AI produced, AI influenced the decision.

That influence must be owned.

The blind spot is this:

Organizations talk about trusting AI before defining ownership.

They ask, "Can we trust the model?"

That is not the first question.

The better question is:

Who owns the decision when AI influences the work?

Until that question is answered, trust is only a feeling.

A feeling is not a control.

Trust Is Structure, Not Emotion

In everyday language, trust sounds personal.

"I trust this person."

"I trust this tool."

"I trust the answer."

Business trust is different.

Business trust must be structured.

A company does not trust a financial control because it feels confident. It trusts it because the control has rules, owners, records, checks, thresholds, and escalation paths.

A company does not trust a cybersecurity process because the dashboard looks clean. It trusts it because alerts are classified properly, evidence is reviewed, ownership is assigned, response rules are defined, and decisions can be examined later.

A company does not trust a healthcare administration workflow because a message sounds professional. It trusts it because privacy, patient context, role boundaries, approval rules, and documentation are designed into the process.

AI trust works the same way.

A polished answer is not trust.

A confidence score is not trust.

A clean summary is not trust.

A human saying "looks good" is not trust unless the human has authority, context, evidence, and accountability.

Trust is created when the business defines five things:

Who owns the decision?
What can AI do?
What must a human review?
What evidence must be preserved?
What happens when risk increases or uncertainty appears?

Without these elements, AI may still be useful. But it is not yet trustworthy as part of a business system.

The distinction matters because AI can create confidence faster than it creates accountability.

That is dangerous.

Confidence makes people move.

Accountability makes the movement safe enough to scale.

The Shadow Ledger

Every business already has ledgers.

Finance has ledgers for money. Operations has records for activity. Security has logs for events. Compliance has documentation for controls. Sales has CRM history. Support has ticket records.

But AI creates a new kind of hidden record when it influences decisions without clear ownership.

The Shadow Ledger is the untracked record of operational liability created when AI influences decisions without ownership, boundary rules, or audit trails.

It is "shadow" because it often does not appear in formal reports.

It is a "ledger" because the liability accumulates.

Every time AI influences a customer response without review rules, an entry is added.

Every time AI labels a finance item as routine without a clear owner, an entry is added.

Every time AI summarizes a security alert and the analyst relies on an incomplete version, an entry is added.

Every time AI drafts compliance-sensitive language and nobody records who approved the claim, an entry is added.

Every time AI recommends an action and the organization cannot later explain why the action was taken, an entry is added.

These entries may not show up immediately.

They appear later as rework, disputes, audit gaps, customer complaints, compliance findings, security misses, vendor confusion, employee blame, and executive uncertainty.

The Shadow Ledger grows when organizations treat AI as "only a tool" while letting that tool shape real decisions.

That phrase — "only a tool" — is sometimes true. But it is not enough.

A spreadsheet is also "only a tool." If a flawed spreadsheet drives a financial decision, the organization still owns the decision.

AI is no different.

The business cannot outsource accountability to a model, a vendor, a prompt, a dashboard, or a confidence score.

Ownership must remain visible.

Low, Medium, and High Risk Layers

Not every AI use case needs the same level of control.

That is important.

If every AI activity is treated as high risk, the organization slows down useful adoption. If every AI activity is treated as low risk, the organization creates avoidable exposure.

A practical implementation should separate AI work into risk layers.

Low-risk AI use supports internal thinking, drafting, summarizing, brainstorming, or formatting where mistakes are easy to catch and unlikely to harm customers, finances, operations, compliance, security, or reputation.

Examples include drafting internal meeting notes, creating a first outline, summarizing non-sensitive public material, or generating alternate wording for an internal presentation.

Low-risk does not mean no risk. It means the consequence of error is limited and recoverable.

Medium-risk AI use affects workflow quality, customer communication, operational efficiency, or internal decisions where mistakes may create rework, confusion, customer frustration, or management problems.

Examples include support response drafts, sales account summaries, campaign briefs, invoice classification suggestions, HR policy summaries, or project status reports.

Medium-risk AI requires clearer review standards, assigned owners, and records of important approvals.

High-risk AI use influences money movement, security response, legal or compliance language, healthcare-related administration, employee-impacting decisions, regulated workflows, customer commitments, access control, fraud risk, or executive decisions.

High-risk AI does not necessarily need to be banned.

But it must be designed with stronger boundaries.

AI may assist. AI may prepare evidence. AI may flag patterns. AI may recommend under defined rules. But high-risk decisions need visible ownership, audit trails, escalation paths, and a clear standard for when AI must stop.

The risk layer should determine the decision boundary.

Low-risk work can move faster.

Medium-risk work needs review discipline.

High-risk work needs ownership discipline.

Without this separation, organizations either over-control everything or under-control the one area that can hurt them most.

Decision Velocity

AI can increase output speed without increasing decision speed.

That is one of the most overlooked problems in implementation.

A system may generate summaries, recommendations, classifications, and drafts quickly, but the organization still moves slowly because no one knows what can be trusted, what must be checked, who can approve it, and when it must escalate.

Decision Velocity is the speed at which an organization can move from AI-assisted output to an accountable business decision.

It is not the same as AI response time.

AI response time measures how fast the system produces something.

Decision Velocity measures how fast the organization can use that something responsibly.

A company with high AI speed and low ownership has poor Decision Velocity.

People wait for approvals. Managers recheck work. Compliance asks for missing evidence. Security asks what happened. Finance asks who authorized the exception. Employees hesitate because the tool sounds confident but the boundary is unclear.

The result is strange but common:

AI gets faster, and the organization gets more cautious.

That is not because employees hate innovation.

It is because the system gives them output without enough structure to act.

Decision Velocity improves when AI outputs are connected to owners, risk levels, review standards, and escalation rules.

A low-risk summary may move quickly.

A medium-risk recommendation may require review.

A high-risk action may require approval, evidence, and auditability.

Now the organization can move faster because people know what kind of decision they are handling.

Good boundaries do not slow AI down.

They reduce hesitation.

Audit Trail and Explainability in Plain Business Language

Two phrases often appear in AI governance discussions: audit trail and explainability.

They can sound technical, but the business meaning is simple.

An audit trail answers:

What happened, who approved it, what evidence was used, and when did it occur?

Explainability answers:

Can we understand the main reason the AI output influenced the decision?

Neither concept requires every manager to become a machine learning expert.

A practical audit trail may include the AI output, the source data used, the human reviewer, the approval timestamp, the risk category, any changes made, and the final decision.

A practical explanation may be as simple as:

The invoice was flagged as routine because the vendor matched an approved record, the purchase order matched, the amount was within expected range, and no bank-detail change was detected.

Or:

The ticket was escalated because it involved a privileged user, suspicious login behavior, and a sensitive system.

Or:

The customer message required review because it included a pricing promise, a compliance-sensitive claim, and a nonstandard contract reference.

This is business explainability.

It does not ask the AI to reveal every internal model mechanism.

It asks the workflow to show enough reason for a human, manager, auditor, customer, or regulator to understand why a decision path was followed.

For many business uses, that is the practical requirement.

The organization needs to know what was decided, why it was reasonable, who owned it, and what evidence supported it.

Without that, the Shadow Ledger grows.

The CFO, Risk, and Compliance View

The AI champion often sees usefulness.

The CFO sees cost and liability.

The risk leader sees exposure.

The compliance leader sees documentation gaps.

The general counsel sees accountability.

The cybersecurity leader sees access, data, and incident implications.

All of them are looking at the same AI workflow from different angles.

Their concern is not always resistance. Often, it is pattern recognition.

They know that business problems rarely appear as "the AI made a mistake." They appear as:

Who approved this?
Why was this paid?
Why was this sent to the customer?
Why was this not escalated?
Why was this classified as low risk?
Why was this access granted?
Why was this claim made?
Where is the record?
Who owns the outcome?

If the answer is unclear, the organization has a governance problem.

The CFO does not need every AI workflow to be perfect. But the CFO does need to know whether AI is changing cost behavior, approval risk, audit readiness, control quality, and accountability.

Risk and compliance leaders do not need AI to be avoided. But they need AI to be placed inside a system where high-risk decisions cannot hide behind convenience.

The board does not need a technical lecture. It needs confidence that AI-influenced decisions have ownership, boundaries, evidence, and escalation.

That is the difference between trusting AI and trusting the system around AI.

A Modeled Example: The Invoice That Looked Routine

The following is a modeled example for planning purposes, not an audited client result.

A regional healthcare administration company uses AI to help process vendor invoices.

The goal is reasonable. The finance team handles a high volume of invoices every month. Many are routine. AI is used to extract fields, compare invoices to purchase orders, suggest payment categories, and flag exceptions.

During the pilot, the workflow performs well.

Routine invoices move faster. Field extraction is accurate enough for review. Analysts like the reduced manual typing. Managers see a clear productivity opportunity.

The system is expanded.

For several weeks, the numbers look good.

Then an invoice from an existing vendor enters the workflow. The vendor name matches. The amount is within a normal range. The invoice format looks familiar. The AI marks the item as routine.

But one detail is different: the payment instructions have changed.

The analyst sees the routine label and reviews quickly. The manager approves the batch. The payment is scheduled.

Later, finance discovers the bank-detail change should have triggered additional verification.

The problem is not that AI formally approved the invoice.

It did not.

The problem is that AI influenced the review path.

The "routine" label lowered attention.

The workflow had no clear rule that payment-detail changes must override routine classification.

The approval record showed that a human approved the batch, but it did not show whether the human reviewed the changed payment details.

The audit trail was incomplete.

The decision boundary was weak.

The Shadow Ledger had been growing quietly.

The organization redesigns the workflow.

First, it separates low-risk invoice extraction from high-risk payment approval.

AI may extract fields and compare routine values.

AI may suggest categories.

AI may not classify an invoice as routine if payment instructions, vendor banking details, tax information, address, ownership, unusually rushed timing, or approval path changes.

Second, the system adds a risk layer.

Low-risk invoices can move through standard review.

Medium-risk invoices require analyst review with required fields checked.

High-risk invoices require separate verification before payment approval.

Third, the approval record changes.

For high-risk invoices, the system must record the exception trigger, the reviewer, the verification step, the final approver, and the decision time.

Fourth, the AI output changes language.

Instead of saying "routine," it says:

"No exception detected in standard fields" or "Exception detected: payment-detail change requires verification."

That wording matters.

It prevents the AI from sounding more certain than the workflow allows.

The result is not slower finance.

It is safer finance.

Routine invoices still move faster. High-risk invoices receive the attention they deserve. Managers have better records. The CFO has a stronger control story. Compliance has cleaner evidence. Employees have less ambiguity.

The company did not solve the problem by "trusting AI more."

It solved the problem by trusting a better-designed decision system.

Confidence Is Not a Boundary

AI systems often produce confident language.

That confidence can be useful when the task is low risk and the user understands the context.

It becomes dangerous when confidence substitutes for a boundary.

A confident summary is not approval.

A confident classification is not ownership.

A confident recommendation is not authorization.

A confident draft is not a verified claim.

A confident risk label is not a control.

The more polished the AI output becomes, the more important boundaries become.

Why?

Because humans are influenced by fluent language.

A clean summary feels reviewed. A well-structured recommendation feels reasoned. A precise answer feels authoritative. A green label feels safe.

But fluent output can still be incomplete.

That is why ownership matters more than confidence.

The business must decide where AI may assist, where it may recommend, where it may act, where it must escalate, and where it must stop.

These boundaries are not anti-AI.

They are what make useful AI safe enough to use.

How to Reduce the Shadow Ledger

The Shadow Ledger shrinks when AI influence becomes visible.

Start by naming the decision AI touches.

Not the task.

The decision.

Does AI influence what gets paid, sent, escalated, approved, classified, prioritized, investigated, promised, rejected, or ignored?

Then name the owner.

A workflow owner must be accountable for the business outcome. A technical owner may manage the system. A reviewer may check the output. But the business decision still needs a business owner.

Next, define the risk layer.

Is this low, medium, or high risk?

Then define the boundary.

Can AI assist, recommend, act under narrow rules, escalate, or stop?

Then preserve evidence.

What must be recorded so the organization can explain the decision later?

Finally, define escalation.

What conditions require human review, manager approval, compliance input, security escalation, legal review, or immediate stop?

This does not require a giant bureaucracy.

It requires clear thinking.

The more important the decision, the more visible the ownership must be.

The Real Lesson

AI trust is not created by confidence.

It is created by design.

A business system can use AI responsibly when decisions have owners, risk layers, boundaries, audit trails, and escalation rules.

Without those structures, AI influence becomes hard to see and harder to govern.

That is how the Shadow Ledger grows.

The organization may not notice it at first. The workflow may look faster. The output may look cleaner. The pilot may look successful. But if AI is shaping decisions without ownership, the risk is accumulating somewhere.

Eventually, someone asks:

Who decided this?

If the organization cannot answer, it has already lost control of the decision.

The answer is not to avoid AI.

The answer is to make AI influence visible.

Trust the system, not the feeling.

Design the ownership before scaling the confidence.

That is how AI becomes usable inside real business systems.

Decision Architect's Field Notes

What to Do Next

Choose one AI workflow that influences a real business decision.

Do not start by asking whether the AI output is accurate. Start by asking who owns the outcome.

Write down the decision AI influences. For example: classify the invoice, route the ticket, draft the customer response, prioritize the alert, approve the exception, recommend the campaign claim, or summarize the patient administration record.

Then assign the workflow to a risk layer: low, medium, or high.

Low-risk work can move quickly with light review. Medium-risk work needs defined review standards and a named owner. High-risk work needs stronger approval, evidence, escalation, and audit trail requirements.

Next, define the boundary.

Can AI assist, recommend, act under narrow rules, escalate, or stop?

Finally, decide what record must be kept. At minimum, high-risk AI-influenced decisions should preserve the AI output, the human reviewer, the evidence used, the final decision, and the approval time.

Common Traps to Avoid

Do not confuse confidence with trust.

Do not say "AI did not decide" if people acted because of what AI produced.

Do not let a human reviewer become a rubber stamp.

Do not treat all AI use cases as the same risk level.

Do not allow high-risk decisions to move through low-risk workflows.

Do not rely on vendor confidence scores as a substitute for business ownership.

Do not wait for an audit, incident, complaint, or financial error to discover that no one owns the AI-influenced decision.

Boardroom Question

Where is AI already influencing business decisions without a named owner, defined boundary, audit trail, or escalation rule?

Industry Translation

In finance, the Shadow Ledger appears when AI labels invoices, vendors, payments, or exceptions without clear approval ownership.

In cybersecurity, it appears when AI summarizes or prioritizes alerts but no one owns the escalation decision or response threshold.

In healthcare administration, it appears when AI drafts, summarizes, or classifies sensitive records without clear role boundaries and documentation.

In marketing and GTM, it appears when AI-generated claims influence public messaging without proof ownership, legal review, or brand accountability.

In MSP and IT services, it appears when AI routes or downgrades tickets without clear escalation rules for security-sensitive or business-critical issues.

Implementation Law

Unowned AI decisions do not disappear. They accumulate.

Part II - Redefining AI Strategy

Chapter 6 - The Death of Tool-Based Thinking

Why Tools Do Not Create Strategy

The executive team had finally made a decision.

After months of internal discussion, they approved a suite of AI tools for the company. One tool for writing. One for meetings. One for customer support. One for sales research. One for code assistance. One embedded inside the CRM. One added to the help desk. One connected to analytics.

The rollout looked organized.

Licenses were purchased. Training sessions were scheduled. Department heads received access. The internal announcement sounded confident: the company was now moving aggressively into AI.

For the first few weeks, usage increased.

Marketing created more drafts. Sales generated prospecting emails. Support summarized tickets. Managers summarized meetings. Analysts asked AI to prepare reports. Employees experimented with prompts. A few early adopters became internal champions.

Then the harder questions arrived.

Which workflow had improved?

Which decision was now better?

Which customer outcome had changed?

Which costs had gone down?

Which risks had gone up?

Which outputs could be trusted?

Which departments were using AI safely?

Which projects deserved scale?

No one had a clean answer.

The company had bought tools.

It had not built strategy.

That is the death of tool-based thinking.

The blind spot is this:

Organizations confuse tool access with AI strategy.

They assume that if the right software is available, implementation will naturally follow. It usually does not.

A tool can help people work differently. It can reduce friction. It can expand capability. It can make certain tasks faster. It can open new possibilities.

But a tool does not decide what the business should improve.

A tool does not define the workflow.

A tool does not assign ownership.

A tool does not decide which risks are acceptable.

A tool does not create evidence.

A tool does not prove business value.

Software can enable AI adoption.

It cannot replace implementation strategy.

Why Tool-First Thinking Fails

Tool-first thinking begins with the wrong question.

It asks:

"What AI tool should we use?"

That question is not useless. Eventually, the organization must choose tools. But as the first question, it is too shallow.

A better first question is:

"What business decision or workflow must become better?"

That question changes everything.

If the organization starts with the tool, every problem begins to look like a place to insert the tool. Marketing asks for content generation. Sales asks for email drafting. Support asks for ticket summaries. Finance asks for document extraction. HR asks for job descriptions. IT asks for automation.

Some of those uses may be helpful.

But helpful is not the same as strategic.

Tool-first thinking fails because it treats AI as an object to deploy instead of a capability to design into work.

The tool-first organization asks:

Can AI do this task?

The decision-first organization asks:

Should AI influence this decision, under what boundary, with what evidence, and who owns the result?

The first question produces activity.

The second question produces implementation.

This distinction is the bridge from Part I to Part II.

The earlier chapters showed how speed, activity, rework, pilots, and trust can mislead leaders when the decision layer is missing. Tool-based thinking is the root habit underneath many of those blind spots.

It keeps the conversation at the software level.

But AI implementation lives at the business-system level.

Vendor Demos Create False Confidence

Vendor demos are often useful.

They show what a product can do. They help teams imagine possibilities. They make abstract capabilities visible. They reduce fear. They create momentum.

The problem is not the demo.

The problem is what leaders sometimes believe the demo has proven.

A demo usually shows the tool under favorable conditions. The data is clean. The use case is selected. The workflow is simplified. The output is polished. The presenter knows where the product performs well. The risks are usually handled in a controlled way.

That is normal.

A demo is designed to show possibility.

It is not designed to prove production value.

A demo can show that AI can summarize tickets.

It does not prove that the support workflow will reduce resolution time after review, escalation, client context, and exceptions are counted.

A demo can show that AI can write campaign copy.

It does not prove that buyers will trust the message, sales will use it, legal will approve it, or pipeline quality will improve.

A demo can show that AI can classify invoices.

It does not prove that payment risk, vendor changes, audit trails, and approval rules are properly controlled.

A demo can show that AI can analyze cybersecurity alerts.

It does not prove that analysts can rely on the output for severity decisions, containment actions, or escalation.

Vendor demos create false confidence when leaders mistake capability for fit.

Capability means the tool can perform a function.

Fit means the tool improves a real workflow inside the organization's constraints.

Those are different standards.

A serious AI strategy uses vendor demos as discovery, not proof.

The right response after a good demo is not, "Let's roll this out."

The right response is:

"Which specific workflow should we test, what decision will this support, what evidence will prove improvement, and what boundary must exist before scale?"

That is how a demo becomes useful without becoming dangerous.

Software Is Necessary but Insufficient

This chapter is not an argument against software.

AI tools matter.

Good software can reduce friction, improve quality, expand access, increase speed, support analysis, organize information, and make new workflows possible.

A weak tool can damage adoption. A poorly integrated tool can create frustration. A vendor with poor security, weak support, unclear pricing, or limited auditability can create problems no strategy can fully hide.

Tool quality matters.

But tool quality is not the whole strategy.

A strong AI tool placed into a weak business system will often amplify confusion.

If the workflow is unclear, the tool accelerates unclear work.

If ownership is unclear, the tool spreads accountability gaps.

If the data is messy, the tool produces polished uncertainty.

If the decision boundary is undefined, the tool invites overuse.

If measurement is weak, the tool creates stories instead of evidence.

If risk levels are not separated, the tool treats routine work and sensitive work too similarly.

Software is the engine.

Strategy is the road, the traffic rules, the destination, the driver, the maintenance plan, and the decision about where the vehicle should not go.

An engine matters.

But an engine alone is not transportation strategy.

The same is true with AI.

Decision-First Strategy

A decision-first AI strategy begins before tool selection.

It starts with the business system.

What workflow matters enough to improve?

What decision inside that workflow creates cost, delay, risk, customer friction, quality problems, or lost opportunity?

Who owns that decision today?

What information does the decision require?

What goes wrong when the decision is delayed, weak, inconsistent, or poorly documented?

What part of the work could AI assist, recommend, act on, or escalate?

What risk layer applies?

What evidence would prove the workflow improved?

Only after those questions are answered does tool selection become meaningful.

Now the organization is not shopping for "AI."

It is selecting capability for a defined implementation problem.

That difference is large.

A tool-first strategy says:

"We bought AI writing software. Where can we use it?"

A decision-first strategy says:

"Our sales team loses time preparing account-specific follow-up after discovery calls. We need AI to help convert approved call notes, buyer pain points, objections, and product proof into a first-draft follow-up that the account owner reviews before sending."

That second statement is stronger because it defines the workflow, the user, the decision, the inputs, the boundary, and the review role.

The tool may still matter.

But the tool is now serving a strategy.

It is no longer pretending to be the strategy.

A Focused Example: Marketing/GTM Without Tool-Based Thinking

A B2B company wants to use AI in marketing and GTM.

The tool-first version is predictable.

The company approves an AI writing tool and tells the marketing team to use it for blogs, emails, LinkedIn posts, landing pages, webinar descriptions, and sales scripts.

Output increases.

The first month looks productive.

Then the problems begin.

The content sounds polished but generic. The sales team says the messaging does not reflect real buyer conversations. The CEO says the company sounds like everyone else. Legal flags unsupported claims. Campaign volume rises, but qualified response does not. The team is now editing more than expected.

The tool worked.

The strategy did not.

A decision-first approach would begin differently.

The company asks:

"What GTM decision are we trying to improve?"

The answer is not "write more content."

The better answer is:

"We need to improve how quickly and consistently we turn real buyer insight into credible campaign briefs for specific market segments."

That is a more strategic use case.

Now the workflow can be designed.

Inputs include approved positioning, customer objections, sales-call notes, proof points, case evidence, competitive differentiation, product limitations, and compliance constraints.

AI's role is not to "create content."

AI's role is to prepare a structured first-draft campaign brief.

The human marketing owner reviews the brief for buyer relevance, proof strength, claim accuracy, and brand fit.

Sales reviews whether the message reflects real conversations.

Legal reviews only if the brief includes regulated or high-risk claims.

The output is not measured by volume alone.

It is measured by sales acceptance, campaign readiness, message quality, reduction in drafting time after review, and improvement in buyer-specific relevance.

Now AI has a business job.

It helps the team make a better GTM decision:

What should we say, to whom, based on what proof, for what next action?

The tool still matters. A weak tool may not handle the workflow well. A better tool may support templates, approved sources, collaboration, and traceability.

But the value comes from the decision design.

Without that design, the same tool becomes a content inflation machine.

With that design, it becomes a GTM leverage system.

That is the difference between tool use and strategy.

The Tool Stack Is Not the Operating Model

Many organizations proudly build an AI stack.

They list platforms, licenses, integrations, model access, plugins, assistants, automation tools, analytics tools, and workflow features.

The stack may be impressive.

But the stack is not the operating model.

An operating model defines how work gets done.

It defines who owns decisions, how work moves, what standards apply, what gets measured, what risks require escalation, and how improvement is governed.

AI tools must fit into that operating model.

If the operating model is missing, the stack becomes a pile of capabilities looking for discipline.

This is why some organizations spend heavily on AI and still struggle to explain results.

They can describe what they bought.

They cannot describe what changed.

A practical AI strategy should be able to answer:

Which workflows are priority?

Which decisions are being improved?

Which roles are changing?

Which controls are required?

Which measures prove value?

Which pilots deserve scale?

Which projects should stop?

Which tools support the design?

The last question matters.

It is not the first question.

The New Buying Standard

Tool-based thinking also damages vendor evaluation.

If the organization does not know the workflow, it cannot properly evaluate the tool.

Everything becomes a feature comparison.

Which product has more integrations?

Which model is more advanced?

Which demo looks better?

Which interface feels easier?

Which vendor says "enterprise-ready" more convincingly?

Those factors may matter, but they are not enough.

A decision-first buying standard asks vendors harder questions:

How does your tool support our specific workflow?

How does it preserve evidence?

How does it handle exceptions?

How does it show uncertainty?

How does it support human review?

How does it log actions?

How does it separate users, roles, and permissions?

How does pricing behave at production volume?

How does the tool fail?

What should we not use it for?

That last question is especially useful.

A serious vendor should be able to explain where the product fits and where it does not.

If every use case is presented as a perfect fit, the buyer should become more cautious.

Good AI strategy improves buying judgment.

It prevents the organization from purchasing a tool because it looks intelligent and then discovering that it does not fit the real workflow.

The Transition From Tools to Decision Architecture

Part II begins here because the organization cannot fix AI implementation blind spots with more tools alone.

Tools are necessary.

They are not enough.

The real shift is from tool-based thinking to Decision Architecture.

Decision Architecture is the discipline of designing how decisions move through a business system when humans and AI operate together.

That discipline requires a new kind of role.

Not merely a prompt writer.

Not merely a software buyer.

Not merely an innovation champion.

Not merely a project manager.

The organization needs someone who can connect workflows, decisions, evidence, ownership, risk, economics, and AI capability into a practical implementation path.

That is the AI Strategist as Decision Architect.

Chapter 7 will define that role.

For now, the lesson is simple.

Do not begin with the tool.

Begin with the decision the tool must improve.

Decision Architect's Field Notes

What to Do Next

Pick one AI tool your organization has already approved or is considering.

Do not start by listing features.

Start by writing one sentence:

"This tool should improve the decision to ___________ inside the workflow of _________."

If you cannot complete that sentence clearly, the tool is not yet attached to strategy.

Next, identify the owner of the workflow, the users who will touch the tool, the risk level of the decision, and the evidence that would prove improvement.

Then ask whether the tool supports that design.

If it does, continue evaluation.

If it does not, either redesign the use case or stop treating the tool as strategic.

Common Traps to Avoid

Do not confuse licenses with implementation.

Do not treat a vendor demo as proof of business value.

Do not buy AI software before defining the workflow and decision it must improve.

Do not let departments choose tools independently without shared standards for ownership, evidence, risk, and measurement.

Do not assume the best model automatically creates the best business result.

Do not mistake a tool stack for an operating model.

Do not ask only what the tool can do. Ask what it should not do inside your business.

Boardroom Question

Which AI tools have we approved or purchased without clearly defining the workflow, decision, owner, boundary, risk level, and evidence of value?

Industry Translation

In marketing and GTM, tool-based thinking creates more content. Decision-first strategy improves buyer-specific messaging, proof quality, sales acceptance, and campaign decisions.

In MSP and IT services, tool-based thinking adds AI features to ticketing. Decision-first strategy defines which tickets AI can summarize, recommend, route, escalate, or stop.

In operations, tool-based thinking automates tasks. Decision-first strategy identifies where delay, defects, handoffs, exceptions, or approvals actually constrain throughput.

In finance, tool-based thinking buys document extraction. Decision-first strategy separates routine processing from approval risk, audit evidence, and exception handling.

The next question is not which tool to buy, but who inside the organization is capable of connecting AI capability to workflow reality, decision ownership, risk, and measurable value.

Implementation Law

A tool can enable AI adoption. It cannot replace implementation strategy.

Chapter 7 - The AI Strategist as a Decision Architect

The Real Role Behind Practical AI Implementation

The company had no shortage of AI activity.

IT had approved several tools. Marketing had a writing assistant. Sales had an AI feature inside the CRM. Customer support had ticket summaries. Finance was testing document extraction. Cybersecurity was reviewing alert summarization. HR had experimented with job descriptions and onboarding content. A few vendors were already involved. Several pilots were moving.

On the surface, the organization looked active.

Then the COO asked a simple question:

"Who is connecting all of this to actual business decisions?"

The answer was uncomfortable.

IT owned access and security review.

Department managers owned their local experiments.

Vendors owned their product demos.

Power users owned their prompts.

Finance watched cost.

Legal watched risk.

Executives watched progress updates.

But no one owned the decision design.

No one was mapping which workflows mattered most. No one was identifying the decisions AI should improve. No one was measuring whether the AI-assisted workflow created real net gain. No one was defining where AI could assist, recommend, act, escalate, or stop. No one was translating AI activity into financial language the CFO could trust.

The organization had tool owners.

It had pilot owners.

It had vendor owners.

It did not have an AI Strategist acting as a Decision Architect.

That is the blind spot.

Organizations assign AI responsibility to tool owners or technical teams, but fail to assign decision architecture responsibility.

This is why many AI initiatives become scattered. The tools may be real. The pilots may be useful. The vendors may be capable. But the system still lacks the person or function responsible for connecting AI capability to workflow reality, decision ownership, risk, evidence, and measurable value.

That is the real role of the AI Strategist.

The AI Strategist as Decision Architect

An AI Strategist is not simply someone who knows AI tools.

An AI Strategist is the person who helps an organization decide where AI should be used, how it should be used, who should own the outcome, what risks must be controlled, what evidence proves value, and whether the initiative deserves scale.

In this book, the strongest version of that role is the AI Strategist as Decision Architect.

A Decision Architect designs how decisions move through a business system when humans and AI work together.

That definition matters.

AI implementation is not only about automation. It is about changing how work is judged, routed, reviewed, approved, escalated, and measured.

The AI Strategist must therefore understand both sides of the equation:

AI capability and business consequence.

A model may summarize. But what decision does the summary support?

A tool may classify. But who owns the classification?

A system may recommend. But what evidence is required before action?

An agent may execute steps. But where must it stop?

A workflow may become faster. But did the business result improve after review, correction, risk, and cost are counted?

These are not narrow technical questions.

They are implementation questions.

The AI Strategist as Decision Architect exists to ask them before scale, not after failure.

What the Role Is Not

The AI Strategist role is often misunderstood because the market uses the phrase loosely.

Some people use it to mean prompt expert.

Some use it to mean AI tool buyer.

Some use it to mean innovation evangelist.

Some use it to mean technical project manager.

Each of those skills can be useful.

None of them is enough.

An AI Strategist is not just a prompt writer.

Prompting can matter. A well-written prompt can improve output. But prompt quality alone does not define workflow ownership, risk level, audit trail, production cost, customer impact, or business value. A company cannot prompt its way out of unclear decisions.

An AI Strategist is not just a tool buyer.

Tool selection matters, but tools do not create strategy by themselves. Buying more AI software without defining the workflow and decision only expands the surface area of confusion.

An AI Strategist is not just an innovation cheerleader.

Optimism helps adoption, but cheerleading cannot replace evidence. A serious AI Strategist must be able to say yes, no, not yet, redesign, or stop.

An AI Strategist is not just an IT project manager.

IT is essential. Security, integration, access control, data handling, vendor review, and technical operations matter. But AI implementation also requires business judgment, financial translation, workflow design, human adoption, risk interpretation, and decision ownership.

The role may work closely with IT.

It should not be reduced to IT.

The AI Strategist sits between business, technology, finance, risk, operations, and human behavior.

That is why the role is valuable.

It connects pieces that usually remain separate.

What the Role Actually Does

The AI Strategist as Decision Architect does several practical jobs.

First, the role acts as a workflow analyst.

This means studying how work actually moves through the organization. Not how the process looks in a slide deck. How it happens in real life. Where work waits. Where handoffs fail. Where employees use spreadsheets outside the system. Where customers get delayed. Where managers recheck work. Where exceptions pile up.

AI should not be aimed at vague goals like "improve operations" or "make marketing faster." It should be aimed at specific workflow friction.

Second, the role acts as a decision mapper.

Every serious workflow contains decisions. What should be approved? What should be escalated? What should be sent? What should be classified? What should be investigated? What should be ignored? What should be stopped?

The AI Strategist identifies those decisions and asks which ones AI should support.

Third, the role acts as a risk translator.

AI risk should not be discussed only in abstract language. The strategist translates risk into business terms: customer harm, financial exposure, compliance gap, operational disruption, security failure, brand damage, audit weakness, employee confusion, or decision ambiguity.

This helps leaders decide what level of control is appropriate.

Fourth, the role acts as an evidence builder.

A serious AI initiative needs proof. The strategist helps define the baseline, measure the AI-assisted workflow, count review and correction, document exception handling, and prepare the evidence needed for a scale-or-stop decision.

Fifth, the role acts as a financial translator.

Executives do not need poetic claims about transformation. They need to understand cost, capacity, margin, cycle time, risk reduction, throughput, customer impact, and return on effort. The strategist helps translate AI activity into economic language.

Sixth, the role acts as a human/AI boundary designer.

This is one of the most important responsibilities.

The strategist helps define what AI can do alone, what it can recommend, what must be reviewed, what should escalate, and what should remain human-owned.

Without this boundary, AI either gets underused because people distrust it or overused because people assume it is safer than it is.

Seventh, the role acts as an implementation communicator.

AI implementation changes how people work. The strategist must explain the "why" and the "how" in plain language. Employees need to understand what AI is doing, what it is not doing, what they still own, when they should trust the output, and when they should challenge it.

If people do not understand the operating model, adoption becomes uneven and risky.

Why This Role Matters for Companies

Companies need this role because AI creates a coordination problem.

AI touches many parts of the business at once. A single workflow can involve operations, IT, data, security, compliance, finance, legal, customer experience, and frontline employees.

Without a Decision Architect, each group sees only part of the picture.

IT may focus on access and security.

Finance may focus on cost.

Legal may focus on exposure.

Operations may focus on throughput.

Employees may focus on convenience.

Vendors may focus on features.

Executives may focus on speed.

All of these perspectives matter, but they need to be connected.

The AI Strategist helps prevent the organization from confusing local usefulness with enterprise readiness.

A tool may be useful for one team but create risk for another. A pilot may save time for frontline users but increase review burden for managers. A model may perform well in testing but fail when real data, exceptions, and ordinary users enter the workflow.

The Decision Architect does not eliminate complexity.

The role makes complexity visible early enough to manage.

That is a major difference.

Many AI failures are not caused by bad technology alone. They are caused by unmanaged translation between technology and the business system.

The AI Strategist owns that translation.

Why This Role Matters for Career Positioning

The AI Strategist role also matters for individuals.

Many professionals are trying to position themselves in the AI economy. Some believe they need to become machine learning engineers. Some believe they need to master every new tool. Some believe they need to present themselves as AI futurists.

For some careers, deep technical specialization is the right path.

But for many business professionals, consultants, founders, operators, marketers, MSP leaders, finance professionals, cybersecurity professionals, and project leaders, the stronger opportunity is implementation strategy.

The market does not only need people who can use AI.

It needs people who can make AI useful inside real organizations.

That means knowing how to ask better questions:

What workflow matters?

What decision needs improvement?

What business result should change?

What evidence would prove progress?

What risk level applies?

What should AI never do here?

Who owns the outcome?

What happens if the output is wrong?

These questions are valuable because they are scarce.

Many people can generate outputs.

Fewer can design the decision system around those outputs.

That is where serious career positioning begins.

For job seekers, this means an AI Strategist resume should not only say "experienced with AI tools." It should show ability to map workflows, define use cases, evaluate ROI, build evidence, communicate risk, support adoption, and connect AI work to measurable outcomes.

For consultants, it means the offer should not be "AI training" alone. Training may be useful, but the higher-value offer is helping organizations identify where AI should be applied, how to measure it, how to control it, and when to scale or stop.

For recruiters and hiring managers, it means evaluating AI talent differently.

Ask candidates how they would decide whether an AI pilot deserves scale.

Ask how they would measure hidden review cost.

Ask how they would define the boundary between AI and human judgment.

Ask how they would explain AI value to a CFO.

The answers will separate tool users from implementation thinkers.

A Focused Example: Logistics Without a Decision Architect

A mid-sized logistics company decides to modernize its freight routing and exception handling with AI.

The company approves a generative AI copilot for its dispatchers, an AI email assistant for customer updates, and an AI document reader for customs paperwork. Each tool has a local owner. The dispatch manager owns routing. Customer success owns emails. Finance owns customs documents.

At first, everything looks positive. Customer updates are sent faster. Customs documents are summarized quickly. Dispatchers spend less time searching for weather delays.

Then the gaps appear.

Dispatchers begin trusting the AI to suggest alternate routes for delayed trucks, but the AI doesn't understand that certain high-value freight requires specific security protocols. Customer success sends polished emails promising delivery times the AI estimated, without realizing the warehouse hasn't confirmed the stock. Finance blindly approves customs forms that the AI summarized, missing a tariff change that later triggers a massive fine.

The company has tools. It does not have decision architecture.

A Decision Architect would redesign the work.

For routing, the strategist would define the AI's boundary: AI may flag weather delays and recommend alternate routes for standard freight. However, AI must escalate and stop for any freight tagged as high-value, hazardous, or temperature-controlled. A human dispatcher must own that final re-route decision.

For customer updates, the strategist would stop measuring email speed. AI would only be allowed to draft delivery promises using verified, hard data from the warehouse API - never estimating on its own.

For customs paperwork, the strategist would separate low-risk domestic documents from high-risk international tariffs, requiring a human signature for any tariff exception before it is filed.

This is not a larger AI tool project. It is a clearer business implementation. The logistics company does not need an AI Strategist to be the smartest technical person in the room. It needs the AI Strategist to ask the questions that connect technology to freight security, compliance risk, and customer trust. That is the Decision Architect role.

Practical Skills Checklist

A strong AI Strategist does not need to know everything.

But the role does require a practical skill stack.

The person should be able to understand workflows well enough to see where work actually breaks. They should be able to interview employees without turning every conversation into a technology pitch. They should be able to identify decisions inside daily work and separate important decisions from low-value activity.

They should be comfortable with basic AI capabilities and limitations, but they do not need to pretend that every tool is magic. They should know how AI can assist with summarization, classification, drafting, retrieval, analysis, pattern detection, and workflow support. They should also know where AI output requires human review.

They should be able to think in risk layers. Low-risk brainstorming is not the same as payment approval, security escalation, healthcare administration, legal language, or customer-facing claims.

They should understand evidence. That means baseline measurement, AI-assisted measurement, review burden, correction effort, exception handling, and total cost of ownership.

They should be able to communicate with different audiences. Frontline employees need clarity. Executives need business impact. IT needs requirements. Finance needs economic logic. Risk and compliance need controls. Vendors need precise use cases.

They should also be willing to recommend stopping a weak AI project.

That may be the most underrated skill.

A real strategist protects the organization from bad scale.

The Transition to Financial Translation

The AI Strategist as Decision Architect gives AI implementation a center of gravity.

But even strong decision design must eventually face the financial question.

Does the workflow create measurable value?

Does it reduce cost, increase capacity, improve margin, accelerate revenue, protect cash, lower risk, or strengthen enterprise performance?

Executives may appreciate better workflows. They may like cleaner decisions. They may support responsible AI adoption.

But when AI competes for budget, attention, and organizational trust, it must be translated into financial language.

That is where many AI conversations fail.

They describe capability but not value.

They describe time saved but not economic impact.

They describe adoption but not performance.

Chapter 8 moves into that translation layer.

The next question is not only whether AI works.

The next question is whether leaders can connect AI implementation to EBITDA, cash flow, risk-adjusted value, and the financial logic of the business.

Decision Architect's Field Notes

What to Do Next

Look at one AI initiative in your organization and ask who owns the decision design.

Do not ask only who owns the tool.

Ask who owns the workflow, the decision, the boundary, the risk standard, the evidence, and the scale-or-stop recommendation.

If those responsibilities are scattered across people who are not coordinating, the initiative needs Decision Architecture.

A useful first exercise is to write a one-page AI Decision Brief. Include the workflow, decision, AI role, human owner, risk level, required evidence, success measure, and escalation rule.

If the team cannot complete the brief, the project is probably not ready to scale.

Common Traps to Avoid

Do not assume IT alone owns AI implementation.

Do not assume the business unit alone can manage AI risk.

Do not confuse prompt skill with implementation strategy.

Do not hire or assign an AI Strategist who only talks about tools.

Do not let vendors define the business problem for you.

Do not measure the role by the number of pilots launched. Measure it by the quality of the decisions improved and the weak projects stopped before they waste resources.

Boardroom Question

Who is responsible for connecting AI capability to workflow reality, decision ownership, risk control, evidence, and measurable business value?

Industry Translation

In MSP and IT services, the AI Strategist connects ticket workflows, escalation rules, technician workload, client trust, and service economics.

In cybersecurity, the role connects alert summaries, analyst judgment, severity decisions, response ownership, and auditability.

In marketing and GTM, the role connects AI content capability to buyer decisions, proof quality, campaign relevance, sales acceptance, and pipeline impact.

In finance, the role connects document automation to approvals, exception handling, audit trails, payment risk, and cost behavior.

In operations, the role connects process automation to throughput, bottlenecks, handoffs, quality, and production reliability.

Implementation Law

AI strategy becomes real when someone owns the decision design.

Chapter 8 - EBITDA: The Financial Translation Layer

How AI Connects to Financial Outcomes Without Buzzword Abuse

The AI presentation sounded confident.

The team had prepared a clean deck. The pilot had saved time. The tool adoption numbers looked strong. Employees were using AI more often. Several workflows had become faster. The vendor had provided case studies. The internal champion said the company was "building an AI advantage."

Then the CFO asked a question that changed the room.

"How does this show up in the business?"

The team had answers, but not financial answers.

They said AI improved productivity.

The CFO asked, "Did labor cost go down, or did capacity increase?"

They said AI saved time.

The CFO asked, "Was that time redeployed, reduced, or just absorbed into more review?"

They said AI improved service quality.

The CFO asked, "Did churn decrease, resolution time improve, or client satisfaction change?"

They said AI reduced manual work.

The CFO asked, "Did margin improve, throughput increase, risk decrease, or cash flow get better?"

The team had activity.

It had usefulness.

It had stories.

But it did not have financial translation.

That is the blind spot.

Organizations often describe AI value in operational language but fail to translate it into financial language that executives, CFOs, boards, investors, and owners can trust.

This does not mean every AI use case must immediately produce profit.

Some AI work creates learning. Some reduces risk. Some protects capacity. Some improves resilience. Some prepares the organization for future scale.

But if AI is going to compete for budget, leadership attention, vendor spend, employee time, and organizational trust, it must eventually connect to financial logic.

That is where EBITDA becomes useful.

Not as a slogan.

Not as a magic metric.

As a translation layer.

What EBITDA Means in Plain Language

EBITDA stands for Earnings Before Interest, Taxes, Depreciation, and Amortization.

In plain business language, EBITDA is often used as a way to look at operating performance before certain financing, tax, and accounting effects.

For this book, the point is not to turn every reader into an accountant.

The point is simpler:

AI must eventually connect to the operating performance of the business.

That connection can appear in several ways:

AI may reduce operating cost.

AI may increase capacity without adding headcount.

AI may improve gross margin by reducing waste or rework.

AI may accelerate revenue by improving conversion, sales productivity, or customer response.

AI may protect revenue by improving retention, service quality, or risk control.

AI may reduce avoidable losses by preventing errors, fraud, downtime, compliance gaps, or security misses.

AI may improve management visibility so leaders can make better operating decisions.

All of these can matter.

But they are not the same.

A serious AI strategy should not say, "This improves EBITDA" unless it can explain how.

Does it reduce expense?

Does it increase revenue?

Does it protect margin?

Does it reduce risk-adjusted cost?

Does it improve utilization?

Does it increase throughput?

Does it reduce churn?

Does it free scarce expert capacity?

Does it prevent expensive mistakes?

If the answer is vague, the financial claim is weak.

AI strategy becomes more credible when leaders stop using financial language as decoration and start using it as discipline.

Time Saved Is Not Always Money Saved

One of the most common AI ROI mistakes is treating time saved as money saved.

Sometimes time saved does become economic value.

Often it does not.

If AI saves an employee two hours per week, the company has not automatically saved two hours of payroll. The employee is still paid. The benefit depends on what happens next.

Does the employee produce more useful work?

Does the team handle more volume without hiring?

Does cycle time improve?

Does quality improve?

Does a bottleneck disappear?

Does customer response improve?

Does overtime decline?

Does senior review burden fall?

Does risk decrease?

If nothing changes except the employee feels slightly less busy, the improvement may still be good. It may improve morale, reduce fatigue, or create breathing room. But it should not be presented as hard-dollar savings.

This distinction matters because many AI business cases inflate savings.

They calculate time saved, multiply it by hourly cost, and call it ROI.

That may be valid in some high-volume, measurable workflows. It is not valid automatically.

A better financial translation asks:

What changed in the operating system after the time was saved?

For example, if AI helps a support team resolve 15 percent more low-risk tickets with the same staff and without increasing reopen rates, that may create capacity value.

If AI helps a marketing team produce more content but sales rejects the messaging, the time savings may not create business value.

If AI helps finance process routine invoices faster but exceptions still consume expert time, the savings may be smaller than claimed.

If AI helps cybersecurity analysts summarize alerts faster but does not improve escalation quality, the financial story may be risk visibility, not labor savings.

The value is not in the time saved alone.

The value is in what the saved time changes.

The Five Financial Translation Paths

AI value usually connects to finance through five practical paths.

First, cost reduction.

This is the most obvious path, but also the most overclaimed. AI reduces cost only when the organization can remove, avoid, or reduce real expense. That may include less overtime, fewer manual processing hours, lower vendor spend, reduced rework, fewer escalations, or fewer duplicated efforts.

Second, capacity expansion.

This is often more realistic than immediate cost reduction. AI may allow the same team to handle more work without adding headcount. A support team may handle more tickets. A finance team may process more routine documents. A marketing team may prepare more segment-specific campaign briefs. An operations team may monitor more exceptions.

Capacity expansion matters when demand exists and the workflow can absorb the extra capacity.

Third, revenue improvement.

AI can support revenue when it improves speed, relevance, quality, follow-up, targeting, conversion, customer experience, or retention. But revenue claims require care. More outreach is not more revenue. More content is not more pipeline. Faster proposals are not more closed deals unless the sales system actually improves.

Fourth, margin protection.

AI can protect margin by reducing rework, waste, defects, delays, errors, refunds, customer recovery, unnecessary escalations, or inefficient expert usage. This is especially important in service businesses, MSPs, consulting, healthcare administration, finance operations, logistics, and support-heavy organizations.

Fifth, risk-adjusted value.

Some AI projects may not produce obvious short-term profit, but they reduce exposure. They may improve audit readiness, fraud detection, security triage, compliance evidence, exception visibility, or management control.

This value is harder to express, but it can be real.

The key is not to force every AI benefit into the same financial bucket.

The key is to identify which path applies.

Why EBITDA Language Gets Abused

EBITDA language becomes dangerous when leaders use it before the operating logic is clear.

A team says AI will improve EBITDA because it saves time.

But time saved does not automatically improve EBITDA.

A vendor says AI will reduce headcount needs.

But the customer still needs review, exceptions, integration, monitoring, and governance.

A manager says AI will increase productivity.

But productivity is not financial value unless it changes throughput, quality, cost, revenue, margin, or risk.

A consultant says AI will transform operations.

But the CFO needs to know which line of the business changes.

This is not cynicism.

It is financial hygiene.

The CFO is not asking for a perfect forecast. The CFO is asking for the business case to stop floating.

A useful financial translation should answer three questions:

What operating metric changes?

How does that operating metric connect to financial value?

What evidence proves the change after cost and risk are counted?

If the AI initiative cannot answer these questions, it may still be worth testing. But it should not be sold as a financial win.

A Modeled Example: The MSP Margin Claim

The following is a modeled example for planning purposes, not an audited client result.

An MSP tests AI for ticket summarization and routing.

The first report says AI saves four minutes per ticket.

The MSP processes 4,000 tickets per month.

The team calculates:

4 minutes × 4,000 tickets = 16,000 minutes saved.

That equals about 267 hours per month.

The initial claim is:

"AI creates 267 hours of monthly labor savings."

That sounds strong.

But the CFO asks a better question:

"Where does the value show up?"

The team reviews the workflow.

Some savings are real. Low-risk tickets are summarized faster. Technicians spend less time reading long histories. Dispatch becomes quicker for routine issues.

But not all time becomes financial value.

Some of the saved time is absorbed into normal workload. Some is spent reviewing AI classifications. Some is offset by exception handling. Some tickets still require senior technician review. The MSP does not reduce headcount. It does not reduce payroll.

So the team changes the financial claim.

Instead of claiming immediate labor savings, it identifies three value paths.

First, capacity expansion: the same Level 1 team can handle a higher ticket volume without adding staff during normal growth.

Second, margin protection: senior technicians spend less time on low-value triage and more time on higher-value technical work.

Third, service quality: faster initial classification improves response time for routine tickets, which may support retention and client satisfaction.

Now the business case is more honest.

The revised claim is not:

"AI saves 267 hours, therefore EBITDA improves."

The revised claim is:

"AI may improve service margin if routine triage capacity increases, senior review burden falls, and resolution quality does not decline."

That sentence is less flashy.

It is also closer to how a CFO thinks.

The next step is evidence.

The MSP tracks cost per ticket, average handle time, escalation accuracy, reopen rate, senior technician review time, SLA performance, and client satisfaction.

After 60 days, the company can ask:

Did AI reduce the cost of completed service?

Did it improve technician utilization?

Did it protect margin as ticket volume grew?

Did it reduce avoidable escalations?

Did it improve service quality without creating hidden rework?

That is financial translation.

It does not pretend every minute becomes money.

It shows how AI can become measurable business value.

The CFO's AI Questions

A CFO does not need to block AI.

A good CFO can make AI stronger by forcing clearer economic thinking.

The questions are practical:

What cost does this reduce?

What capacity does this create?

What revenue process does this improve?

What margin leak does this close?

What risk does this reduce?

What new cost does this introduce?

What human review does this require?

What happens when usage scales?

What evidence will we accept before expanding?

These questions protect the organization from weak AI math.

They also help strong projects earn support.

An AI project with clear financial translation is easier to fund, easier to govern, easier to defend, and easier to scale.

A project with vague value is vulnerable.

Even if it is useful, it may lose executive support because no one can explain its economic logic.

This is why the AI Strategist must speak financial language.

Not accounting jargon.

Business consequence.

Financial Translation Without Killing Innovation

Some teams worry that financial discipline will slow innovation.

It can, if applied badly.

If every early experiment must prove EBITDA impact immediately, useful discovery will die. Early pilots often create learning before they create financial proof.

But the opposite mistake is also dangerous.

If no project ever has to connect to financial value, the AI portfolio becomes a pile of activity.

The better approach is to match the evidence standard to the stage.

During discovery, the organization can ask:

Is there a real workflow problem here?

During pilot, it can ask:

Can AI improve this workflow under controlled conditions?

During proof, it can ask:

Does the improvement survive review, correction, exception handling, risk, and total cost?

During scale, it must ask:

How does this connect to cost, capacity, revenue, margin, cash, or risk-adjusted value?

This sequence protects innovation and financial discipline at the same time.

Not every idea needs a full business case on day one.

But every idea that asks for scale must eventually face the financial translation layer.

The AI Value Sentence

A practical way to discipline the conversation is to write an AI Value Sentence.

The format is simple:

AI will improve [workflow] by improving [decision or activity], which should affect [operating metric], creating value through [financial path].

For example:

AI will improve support ticket triage by helping classify low-risk tickets faster, which should reduce cost per routine ticket and protect service margin as volume grows.

Or:

AI will improve sales follow-up by turning approved discovery notes into account-specific drafts, which should improve follow-up speed and meeting conversion, creating value through revenue acceleration.

Or:

AI will improve invoice review by flagging exceptions earlier, which should reduce payment risk and audit cleanup, creating value through risk-adjusted cost reduction.

This sentence is not a substitute for measurement.

It is a clarity tool.

If the team cannot write the sentence, the use case is probably too vague.

If the sentence sounds impressive but cannot be measured, the business case is still weak.

If the sentence identifies a real workflow, a real decision, a real operating metric, and a real financial path, the project is ready for better testing.

The Real Lesson

AI value becomes credible when operational improvement can be translated into financial logic.

Not every benefit is EBITDA.

Not every saved minute is cost reduction.

Not every faster workflow improves margin.

Not every risk reduction is easy to quantify.

But every serious AI initiative should be able to explain what kind of value it is trying to create.

The strongest AI conversations do not begin with inflated ROI.

They begin with disciplined translation.

What work changes?

What decision improves?

What cost appears?

What risk changes?

What operating metric moves?

What financial path applies?

What evidence proves it?

That is how AI moves from excitement to credibility.

Chapter 7 defined the AI Strategist as the Decision Architect.

This chapter adds the financial translation layer.

Chapter 9 begins the practical system: diagnosing workflows and extracting the decisions hidden inside them.

Because before AI value can be measured, the work itself must be visible.

Decision Architect's Field Notes

What to Do Next

Choose one AI initiative and write its AI Value Sentence:

AI will improve __________ by improving __________, which should affect __________, creating value through __________.

Then identify which financial path applies: cost reduction, capacity expansion, revenue improvement, margin protection, or risk-adjusted value.

Do not force the project into the wrong category. If the value is capacity, do not call it cost savings. If the value is risk reduction, do not pretend it is immediate revenue. If the value is learning, say that clearly and do not oversell it as ROI.

Next, define one operating metric and one financial logic statement.

The operating metric may be cost per ticket, review time, exception rate, conversion rate, cycle time, capacity per employee, reopen rate, churn risk, audit cleanup time, or utilization.

The financial logic statement should explain how that metric connects to business value.

Common Traps to Avoid

Do not multiply time saved by wages and automatically call it ROI.

Do not use EBITDA language unless you can explain the operating path.

Do not confuse productivity stories with financial evidence.

Do not ignore new AI costs such as review, monitoring, integration, governance, vendor management, and usage growth.

Do not force all AI projects to prove financial impact too early.

Do not allow scaled AI projects to avoid financial translation.

Boardroom Question

Which AI initiatives can we connect to cost, capacity, revenue, margin, cash, or risk-adjusted value — and which are still only described as productivity stories?

Industry Translation

In MSP and IT services, financial translation means connecting AI to cost per ticket, technician utilization, SLA performance, escalation accuracy, client retention, and service margin.

In marketing and GTM, it means connecting AI to campaign quality, sales acceptance, conversion, pipeline relevance, deal velocity, and customer acquisition efficiency.

In finance, it means connecting AI to exception handling, audit readiness, payment risk, processing cost, approval quality, and cash protection.

In cybersecurity, it means connecting AI to analyst leverage, incident triage quality, response time, false-positive handling, business interruption risk, and evidence readiness.

In operations, it means connecting AI to throughput, defects, cycle time, handoff delays, rework, capacity, and margin protection.

Implementation Law

AI value becomes credible when operational improvement can be translated into financial logic.

Part III - The Decision Architecture System

Chapter 9 - Diagnose and Map: Extracting Decisions From Workflows

Why AI Cannot Improve Work the Organization Cannot See

The operations team thought it understood the workflow.

On paper, the process was simple.

A customer request came in. The request was reviewed. Information was gathered. The work was assigned. The task was completed. The customer was updated. The record was closed.

It looked clean enough for automation.

Then the team walked through the actual work.

The request did not always come through one channel. Sometimes it came by email, sometimes by portal, sometimes through a sales rep, sometimes through a phone call, and sometimes through an executive who wanted special handling.

The review step was not one step. It included classification, urgency, customer status, contract terms, technical complexity, risk level, missing information, and the question nobody had written down: "Who will be blamed if this goes wrong?"

The assignment step was not automatic. A coordinator used judgment based on technician skill, client relationship, current workload, informal history, and whether the issue felt riskier than the ticket category suggested.

The customer update was not just communication. It was expectation management.

The record was not simply closed. It was closed only after someone decided the work was complete enough, safe enough, documented enough, and unlikely to reopen.

The process map had shown tasks.

The real workflow contained decisions.

That is the blind spot.

Organizations try to apply AI to workflows before extracting the decisions inside those workflows.

AI cannot improve work the organization cannot see.

It may speed up pieces of the process. It may summarize, draft, classify, retrieve, or recommend. But if the underlying decisions are invisible, AI gets pointed at the wrong problem.

That is why Part III begins with diagnosis and mapping.

Before defining boundaries, designing roles, proving pilots, or deciding what to scale, the organization must first see the work clearly.

Workflows Are Not Just Steps

Most process maps show steps.

Receive request.

Review request.

Assign work.

Complete work.

Update customer.

Close record.

That is useful, but incomplete.

A workflow is not only a sequence of tasks. It is a chain of decisions, handoffs, judgments, exceptions, approvals, and information movements.

The real value often hides between the official steps.

A support ticket may look like a task, but it contains decisions about urgency, category, client impact, security sensitivity, escalation, assignment, and closure.

A marketing campaign may look like content production, but it contains decisions about buyer segment, message, proof, claim risk, offer, timing, channel, and sales handoff.

A finance workflow may look like invoice processing, but it contains decisions about vendor legitimacy, purchase order match, payment risk, approval authority, exception handling, and audit evidence.

A cybersecurity alert may look like triage, but it contains decisions about severity, asset criticality, user privilege, business impact, containment risk, and escalation.

If these decisions are not visible, AI implementation becomes guesswork.

The organization may automate the visible task while leaving the real decision burden untouched.

That is how teams end up with faster summaries but the same bottlenecks, more drafts but weaker messaging, quicker classifications but heavier review, or cleaner dashboards but no better decisions.

Diagnosis begins by separating the workflow into three layers:

What work is performed?

What decision does the work support?

What evidence is needed to make the decision responsibly?

That three-layer view is the foundation of Decision Architecture.

The Decision Extraction Question

The fastest way to diagnose a workflow is to ask one question repeatedly:

"What decision is being made here?"

When someone says, "We review the ticket," ask:

What decision is made during review?

When someone says, "We prepare the report," ask:

What decision does the report support?

When someone says, "We send the customer response," ask:

What decision determines what can be promised?

When someone says, "We approve the invoice," ask:

What decision separates routine payment from exception risk?

This question sounds simple.

It is not always comfortable.

Many organizations discover that important decisions are being made informally by experienced employees without clear rules. That is not necessarily bad. Expert judgment often keeps the business running.

But if the organization wants AI to support the workflow, informal judgment must become visible enough to design around.

AI does not need to replace expert judgment.

But it must know where expert judgment begins.

A practical implementation pattern is to extract decisions in plain language.

For example:

Decide whether this support ticket is low-risk or escalation-required.

Decide whether this invoice can move through routine approval or needs exception review.

Decide whether this marketing claim is supported by approved proof.

Decide whether this security alert is informational, suspicious, or urgent.

Decide whether this customer request fits the contract or requires manager approval.

Each sentence creates a design target.

Now AI can be assigned a role.

It may assist by summarizing.

It may recommend by classifying.

It may act on low-risk cases.

It may escalate unclear or high-risk cases.

It may stop when evidence is missing.

Without the decision sentence, AI has no real job.

Mapping the Workflow Reality

A useful workflow map does not need to be beautiful.

It needs to be honest.

The goal is not to create a consultant diagram. The goal is to reveal how work really moves.

Start with a live workflow, not an idealized process.

Pick one process that happens often enough to matter and has enough friction to justify attention.

Then map six elements.

First, identify the trigger.

What starts the workflow? A ticket, invoice, lead, alert, order, customer request, compliance question, report, claim, renewal, or exception?

Second, identify the actors.

Who touches the work? Frontline employee, manager, analyst, technician, salesperson, finance approver, compliance reviewer, customer, vendor, system, or AI tool?

Third, identify the decisions.

At each step, ask what is being decided. Do not accept vague language such as review, process, handle, assess, or manage. Push until the decision is visible.

Fourth, identify the evidence.

What information is required to make the decision well? Customer history, contract terms, policy, pricing, invoice data, asset criticality, account status, source document, approval record, or risk flag?

Fifth, identify the exceptions.

Where does the workflow break from the normal path? Missing data, unclear ownership, high-risk signals, unusual amounts, VIP customers, unsupported claims, security concerns, compliance issues, or edge cases?

Sixth, identify the outcome.

What does "done" mean? Sent, paid, closed, approved, escalated, resolved, rejected, documented, reviewed, or scheduled?

This map does not need to include every detail. It needs to reveal enough to answer the implementation question:

Where can AI improve the workflow without hiding ownership, increasing risk, or creating more rework?

Do Not Start With the Most Exciting Workflow

Teams often want to start with the most impressive AI use case.

That is not always wise.

The best first workflow for Decision Architecture is usually not the flashiest one. It is the one where the organization can learn quickly, measure honestly, and control risk.

A good first workflow has five traits.

It happens often.

It has visible friction.

It supports a real business outcome.

It has an identifiable owner.

It can be tested without exposing the organization to uncontrolled risk.

This is why workflows such as support triage, invoice exception review, sales follow-up preparation, customer onboarding, campaign briefing, internal reporting, and operational exception summaries often make good early candidates.

They are not trivial.

But they are concrete.

Concrete workflows teach faster than abstract strategy discussions.

The goal is not to find the perfect AI opportunity.

The goal is to build implementation muscle.

Once the organization learns how to diagnose, map, measure, and govern a workflow, it can apply that discipline to more complex use cases.

A Focused Example: Marketing Campaign Briefs

The following is a modeled example for planning purposes, not an audited client result.

A B2B company wants to use AI to improve marketing.

The first idea is broad:

"Use AI to create campaign content."

That is too vague.

A Decision Architect narrows the workflow.

The real workflow is campaign briefing for a new market segment.

Before AI, the marketing manager gathers sales notes, product positioning, customer objections, proof points, competitor claims, and internal assumptions. Then the manager writes a campaign brief. Sales reviews it. Leadership comments. Legal may review claims. The process is slow, and the first draft often misses buyer nuance.

The team maps the workflow.

The trigger is a campaign request for a specific segment.

The actors are marketing, sales, product, legal, and leadership.

The decisions include:

Which buyer problem matters most?

Which segment is the campaign for?

What claim can the company honestly make?

What proof supports the claim?

What objections must the message address?

What call to action fits the buyer's stage?

Which claims require legal review?

What should sales do with the campaign?

Now AI's role becomes clearer.

AI should not simply "write content."

AI can assist by organizing approved inputs.

AI can recommend message angles based on real buyer objections.

AI can identify missing proof.

AI can flag claims that sound unsupported.

AI can draft the first campaign brief using a required structure.

AI should not invent customer results.

AI should not create unapproved competitive claims.

AI should not publish content.

AI should escalate claims involving compliance, regulated industries, pricing promises, or customer outcomes.

The measurement also becomes clearer.

The team does not measure only number of drafts produced. It measures brief completion time, sales acceptance, number of major rewrites, legal review issues, campaign readiness, and eventual campaign performance.

The mapping exercise changes the use case.

The original idea was content generation.

The better use case is decision support for campaign briefing.

That distinction matters.

The company does not need more words.

It needs better marketing decisions.

The Hidden Decisions That Matter Most

Not every decision deserves AI support.

Some decisions are too minor. Some are too risky. Some are too unclear. Some should be redesigned before AI enters.

During diagnosis, the organization should look for decisions with one or more of these traits:

They happen frequently.

They create delays.

They require repetitive information gathering.

They depend on scattered data.

They create inconsistent outcomes.

They consume scarce expert attention.

They cause customer friction.

They create rework.

They hide risk.

They affect revenue, margin, cost, capacity, compliance, or trust.

These are good candidates for deeper analysis.

The strongest AI opportunities often sit where repetitive work and judgment meet.

If the work is purely repetitive and low risk, traditional automation may be enough.

If the work is pure high-stakes judgment, AI may only assist with evidence preparation.

But when a workflow contains repeated decisions that require information gathering, classification, prioritization, drafting, or exception detection, AI may create meaningful leverage.

The key is to understand the decision before choosing the AI role.

Finding the Real Bottleneck

A workflow map should expose the bottleneck.

The bottleneck is the constraint that limits performance.

Sometimes the bottleneck is obvious. A manager must approve every request. A senior technician reviews every classification. A legal reviewer checks every claim. A finance analyst handles every exception.

Sometimes the bottleneck is hidden.

The team thinks writing is slow, but the real bottleneck is proof.

The team thinks ticket triage is slow, but the real bottleneck is escalation uncertainty.

The team thinks invoice processing is slow, but the real bottleneck is exception review.

The team thinks sales follow-up is slow, but the real bottleneck is unclear account strategy.

The team thinks reporting is slow, but the real bottleneck is data trust.

AI should be aimed at the bottleneck, not the most visible task.

This is one reason tool-first thinking fails. A tool may speed up the easiest part of the workflow while leaving the expensive part unchanged.

Diagnosis protects the organization from automating the wrong layer.

Ask:

Where does work wait?

Where do people recheck?

Where do exceptions pile up?

Where does customer trust weaken?

Where do managers intervene?

Where does the same question keep coming back?

Where does unclear ownership slow the process?

Those answers reveal the real AI opportunity.

The Map Should Show What AI Must Not Do

A useful workflow map does not only show where AI can help.

It also shows where AI should not act.

This matters because many AI failures come from overextension. A tool performs well in one step, so the organization lets it influence the next step without enough design.

AI summarizes the ticket, so people trust the classification.

AI drafts the customer response, so people send it with light review.

AI extracts invoice fields, so people assume the payment is routine.

AI summarizes an alert, so people assume severity is low.

The map should prevent that drift.

For each decision, mark AI's possible role:

Assist.

Recommend.

Act under narrow rules.

Escalate.

Stop.

This does not require the full Decision Boundary framework yet. That comes later.

For now, the map should make one thing clear:

AI's role changes depending on the decision and the risk.

A low-risk formatting task may allow AI to act.

A medium-risk customer response may require human review.

A high-risk financial, legal, security, healthcare, or compliance decision may allow AI to prepare evidence but not own the decision.

The map should make these differences visible early.

The Real Lesson

Diagnosis is not a delay tactic.

It is the beginning of real AI implementation.

Organizations that skip diagnosis often automate fragments of work and then wonder why value is weak. They produce more output, but the bottleneck remains. They speed up drafts, but decisions do not improve. They add AI to workflows, but ownership stays unclear.

The purpose of workflow mapping is not to create paperwork.

The purpose is to expose the decisions that determine value.

Once the decisions are visible, AI strategy becomes more practical.

The organization can ask better questions:

Which decision matters most?

Which decision is repetitive enough to support?

Which decision carries risk?

Which decision consumes expert time?

Which decision lacks evidence?

Which decision should AI assist, recommend, act on, escalate, or avoid?

Chapter 8 translated AI into financial logic.

Chapter 9 begins the operating system behind that logic.

Before AI can produce measurable value, the organization must diagnose the workflow, map the decisions, and identify the bottleneck.

The next chapter goes one step deeper.

Once decisions are visible, the organization must extract and prioritize the data, trust, and ROI bottlenecks that determine which AI opportunities deserve attention first.

Decision Architect's Field Notes

What to Do Next

Choose one workflow that is frequent, important, and frustrating.

Do not begin with the AI tool.

Begin with the work.

Write the workflow in plain language from trigger to outcome. Then identify every point where someone makes a decision.

Use direct decision sentences:

Decide whether this request is routine or exception.

Decide whether this claim is supported.

Decide whether this ticket requires escalation.

Decide whether this invoice can move forward.

Decide whether this customer response is safe to send.

Next, write the evidence required for each decision. If the evidence is unclear, scattered, missing, or informal, AI may struggle unless the workflow is redesigned.

Then mark the current bottleneck. Look for waiting, review, rework, escalation, missing information, repeated questions, customer friction, or expert overload.

Finally, assign a preliminary AI role: assist, recommend, act under narrow rules, escalate, or stop.

Common Traps to Avoid

Do not map only the official process. Map how work actually happens.

Do not confuse a task with a decision.

Do not automate the easiest step if the bottleneck is somewhere else.

Do not ignore informal expert judgment. Make it visible enough to design around.

Do not let AI drift from assisting one decision into influencing another without review.

Do not choose the most exciting workflow first if it is too risky, too vague, or too hard to measure.

Boardroom Question

Which business workflows are we trying to improve with AI before we have clearly mapped the decisions, evidence, owners, exceptions, and bottlenecks inside them?

Industry Translation

In MSP and IT services, diagnosis means mapping ticket intake, classification, escalation, assignment, client context, SLA obligations, and closure standards.

In marketing and GTM, it means mapping buyer segment, message, proof, claim risk, sales handoff, campaign readiness, and conversion intent.

In finance, it means mapping document intake, field extraction, exception rules, approval authority, payment risk, audit trail, and cash impact.

In cybersecurity, it means mapping alert intake, enrichment, severity judgment, asset criticality, escalation, response ownership, and evidence preservation.

In operations, it means mapping handoffs, delays, quality checks, exceptions, capacity constraints, approval points, and completion standards.

Implementation Law

A workflow cannot be improved with AI until its decisions are visible.

Chapter 10 - Extract and Prioritize: Finding Data, Trust, and ROI Bottlenecks

Why the Best AI Opportunity Is Usually Not the Loudest One

After the workflow map was finished, the leadership team thought the AI opportunity was obvious.

The process was slow. Employees complained about manual work. Customers waited too long. Managers wanted automation. The vendor demo looked strong.

Then the Decision Architect asked a sharper question:

"Which bottleneck is actually limiting value?"

The answer was not obvious anymore.

The team had mapped the steps, but now it had to find the constraint. Some delays came from missing data. Some came from unclear ownership. Some came from review burden. Some came from exceptions. Some came from low trust in the source system. Some came from approvals that had never been redesigned.

The first AI idea was to automate the visible task.

The better idea was to identify the bottleneck that controlled the economics.

That is the blind spot of this chapter:

Organizations choose AI use cases by visibility, enthusiasm, or tool capability instead of by data readiness, trust readiness, and ROI bottleneck.

The best AI opportunity is not always the task people hate most. It is where AI improves a decision, reduces constraint pressure, and creates measurable value without adding larger hidden cost.

The Three Bottlenecks

After a workflow is mapped, evaluate it through three bottlenecks.

The first is the data bottleneck.

AI needs usable information. If the required data is missing, outdated, scattered, inconsistent, locked in email, buried in notes, or stored in people's heads, AI may produce polished uncertainty. Before scaling, ask: What information does the decision require, where does it live, how reliable is it, and can the system access it safely?

The second is the trust bottleneck.

Some workflows fail because people do not trust the output enough to act. That may happen because the AI gives no source, no reason, no confidence boundary, no exception signal, or no audit trail. If every output needs expert review, the bottleneck may not be generation. It may be trust design.

The third is the ROI bottleneck.

Some AI ideas are useful but not economically important. They save a few minutes in a low-volume workflow. Others touch cost per transaction, capacity, margin, risk, revenue, or customer retention. Prioritization should favor workflows where improvement can change business performance, not just make the demo look impressive.

A strong AI opportunity usually sits where all three overlap: the data is usable enough, trust can be designed, and the financial path is real.

A Practical Prioritization Method

Use a simple scoring conversation before building or buying anything.

For each mapped workflow, rate five questions from 1 to 5:

How painful is the bottleneck?

How frequent is the workflow?

How ready is the data?

How controllable is the risk?

How measurable is the value?

Do not overcomplicate this. The score is not the decision. It is a forcing function.

A workflow with high pain, high frequency, decent data, controlled risk, and measurable value deserves attention.

A workflow with high excitement but poor data, unclear ownership, high risk, and vague value should wait.

The goal is not to kill ambition. The goal is to sequence implementation intelligently.

A Focused Example: Finance Exception Review

The following is a modeled example for planning purposes, not an audited client result.

A finance team wants AI to speed up invoice processing.

The first idea is broad:

"Use AI to process invoices."

The workflow map shows that routine invoices are already handled reasonably well. The real delay comes from exceptions: changed bank details, mismatched purchase orders, new vendors, duplicate invoice signals, missing approvals, and unusual amounts.

The data bottleneck is mixed. Invoice fields are available, but vendor history and approval rules are scattered across systems.

The trust bottleneck is high. Analysts do not want AI to label something safe unless the reason is visible.

The ROI bottleneck is strong. Exceptions consume senior time, delay payment cycles, and create fraud and audit risk.

The redesigned use case becomes narrower and better:

AI will not "approve invoices."

AI will extract fields, compare them against approved records, flag exception reasons, prepare a review packet, and route high-risk items to the right approver.

The implementation advice is specific.

Start with one invoice category and one business unit. Define exception triggers before testing. Require AI to show why an item is routine or risky. Track review time, exception rate, payment delay, duplicate-risk flags, and audit cleanup. Do not allow AI to approve payment-detail changes. Do not average routine invoices and exceptions into one ROI claim.

Now the use case is safer, more measurable, and more valuable.

The team did not choose AI for the whole finance process.

It chose AI for the bottleneck that mattered.

The Real Lesson

Diagnosis shows the workflow. Prioritization shows where to act.

A company should not chase every AI opportunity. It should rank them by business constraint, data readiness, trust design, risk level, and financial logic.

This is where AI strategy becomes practical.

Not:

"Where can we use AI?"

But:

"Where can AI improve a decision that matters, using data we can trust, under risk we can control, with value we can measure?"

That question prevents scattered pilots and protects the organization from expensive enthusiasm.

The next chapter turns this prioritization into the core design tool of the book: the Decision Boundary.

Once the right workflow and decision are chosen, the organization must define what AI can do, what it can recommend, what humans must own, and where the system must stop.

Decision Architect's Field Notes

What to Do Next

Select three mapped workflows. For each one, identify the data bottleneck, trust bottleneck, and ROI bottleneck.

Then score the workflow on pain, frequency, data readiness, risk control, and measurability.

Choose the workflow with the best combination of business value and implementation control. Do not choose the most glamorous one. Choose the one that can teach the organization how to scale correctly.

Common Traps to Avoid

Do not prioritize AI use cases by vendor excitement.

Do not automate a workflow when the real bottleneck is missing data.

Do not scale a workflow that users do not trust enough to act on.

Do not call an AI use case strategic if the value path is vague.

Do not start with high-risk automation when a lower-risk evidence-preparation use case would create faster learning.

Boardroom Question

Which AI opportunities are we prioritizing because they are visible, and which ones actually address the data, trust, and ROI bottlenecks that control business value?

Industry Translation

In finance, prioritize exception review before broad invoice automation.

In MSPs, prioritize ticket escalation accuracy before full routing automation.

In cybersecurity, prioritize evidence preparation before automated response.

In marketing and GTM, prioritize campaign decision quality before content volume.

In operations, prioritize bottlenecks that control throughput, defects, or capacity.

Implementation Law - AI should be prioritized where data, trust, and measurable value meet.

Chapter 11 - Define: The Human vs. AI Decision Boundary Framework

What AI Can Do, What Humans Must Own, and Where the System Must Stop

The team finally chose the right workflow.

The data was good enough. The bottleneck was real. The business value was measurable. The pilot had a clear owner.

Then the project almost failed for a different reason.

Nobody had defined the boundary.

Employees did not know when AI could act, when it could recommend, when they had to review, or when the system had to escalate. Managers said, "Use judgment." Risk said, "Keep a human involved." IT said, "The tool is configurable." The vendor said, "The workflow supports approvals."

None of that was enough.

The workflow needed a decision boundary.

The blind spot is this:

Organizations ask what AI can do before defining what AI is allowed to do.

A Decision Boundary defines what AI can do alone, what it can recommend, what must be reviewed, and what should remain human-owned.

This is the practical center of AI implementation.

Without a boundary, AI becomes either too weak to matter or too loose to trust.

The Four AI Roles

A useful boundary starts with four roles.

Assist means AI helps a human work faster or see more clearly. It may summarize, draft, organize, extract, compare, or prepare evidence. The human still owns the decision.

Recommend means AI suggests a classification, next step, priority, message, route, or action. A human reviews the recommendation before it changes the workflow.

Act means AI performs a narrow action under predefined rules. This should be limited to low-risk, repeatable, well-defined situations with monitoring.

Escalate means AI sends the work to a human, manager, specialist, compliance reviewer, security analyst, or stop path because risk, uncertainty, missing data, or exception signals are present.

A fifth word is also needed:

Stop.

Stop means AI should not proceed. The system should pause when the decision is too risky, the evidence is missing, or the request is outside the approved boundary.

Three Decision Types

Not all decisions are the same.

Deterministic decisions follow clear rules. For example, "If the invoice amount is under the approved threshold and all fields match, route to standard review."

Probabilistic decisions involve likelihood. For example, "This ticket appears likely to be a password reset," or "This alert resembles prior suspicious behavior."

Judgment-based decisions require business context, ethics, trust, reputation, legal interpretation, customer nuance, or risk ownership. For example, "Should we promise this outcome to a customer?" or "Should we contain this security event?"

The more judgment a decision requires, the more careful the boundary must be.

Compact Boundary Guide

Use this as the working version. Expanded versions belong in the Toolkit.

A Decision Boundary should be simple enough for managers, analysts, technicians, marketers, and executives to use without a large table.

Start with the decision type.

1. Deterministic Decisions

These decisions follow clear rules: thresholds, required-field matches, routing rules, duplicate checks, or approved categories.

AI can usually assist or recommend here. It may act only when the risk is low, the rule is clear, and the outcome is easy to monitor.

AI should escalate or stop when rules conflict, required data is missing, or the case falls outside the approved pattern.

2. Probabilistic Decisions

These decisions involve likelihood, pattern recognition, or confidence rather than certainty.

AI can usually assist. It may recommend, but the recommendation should normally be reviewed before it changes the workflow.

AI should rarely act on its own, except in narrow, low-risk situations with clear monitoring. It should escalate or stop when uncertainty is high, context is missing, or the result could affect money, security, compliance, customers, or reputation.

3. Judgment-Based Decisions

These decisions require business context, ethics, trust, legal interpretation, customer nuance, security responsibility, or executive accountability.

AI can assist by preparing evidence, summaries, options, comparisons, or draft language.

AI may recommend only with clear human review and visible supporting evidence. It should not act on its own in most judgment-based decisions.

AI should escalate or stop when human ownership, legal review, compliance review, financial approval, security judgment, or customer-trust protection is required.

This guide prevents one major mistake: treating every AI-supported decision as if it belongs in the same automation lane. Deterministic decisions may allow controlled automation. Probabilistic decisions usually require review. Judgment-based decisions must remain human-owned, even when AI helps prepare the evidence.

Applying the Boundary

For an MSP, AI may assist by summarizing all tickets. It may recommend categories for routine tickets. It may act by routing a narrow class of low-risk password reset requests. It must escalate tickets involving security language, executive users, backup failure, identity risk, outages, or missing client context.

For cybersecurity, AI may assist by summarizing alerts and gathering evidence. It may recommend severity for analyst review. It should not independently decide to ignore high-risk incidents or trigger disruptive containment without defined controls. It must escalate when privileged users, sensitive assets, lateral movement, or repeated signals appear.

For finance, AI may assist by extracting invoice fields. It may recommend routine or exception status. It may act only on low-risk routing, not payment approval. It must escalate changed bank details, new vendors, duplicate signals, missing purchase orders, unusual amounts, or rushed payment requests.

The boundary is not anti-AI.

It lets AI work where it fits and protects the business where judgment matters.

How to Implement the Boundary Correctly

Start with one decision sentence.

"Decide whether this invoice is routine or exception."

"Decide whether this ticket can be routed automatically."

"Decide whether this alert needs analyst escalation."

Then define the AI role for that decision.

Do not define the role for the whole workflow. Define it for each decision inside the workflow.

Next, define risk triggers.

Risk triggers are conditions that change AI's role. A low-risk ticket may be routable until it mentions suspicious login activity. A routine invoice may move forward until payment details change. A marketing draft may be usable until it makes a claim requiring proof.

Then define evidence requirements.

If AI recommends something, what must it show? Source record, matching rule, confidence note, exception flag, missing data, or reason for escalation?

Then define the human owner.

The owner is not "the team." The owner is the role accountable for the decision outcome.

Finally, test the boundary on real cases. Use normal cases, messy cases, and edge cases. If employees disagree about what AI is allowed to do, the boundary is not clear enough.

Blank Template

Use this compact template for every AI-supported decision:

Decision:
AI role: assist / recommend / act / escalate / stop
Decision type: deterministic / probabilistic / judgment-based
Risk level: low / medium / high
Human owner:
Required evidence:
Escalation triggers:
What AI must not do:
Success measure:

This template is short by design.

If the team cannot complete it, the use case is not ready.

The Real Lesson

A Decision Boundary turns AI from a tool into an operating discipline.

It gives employees clarity. It gives managers control. It gives risk leaders evidence. It gives CFOs cleaner economics. It gives executives a reason to trust scale.

The boundary does not remove human judgment.

It protects it from being buried under machine-generated confidence.

How to Use the Decision Boundary in a Real Meeting

Most teams make the Decision Boundary harder than it needs to be.

They turn it into a policy discussion, a vendor argument, or a vague governance conversation about keeping "a human in the loop." None of that helps a working team decide what AI may do on Monday morning.

A real boundary meeting should be short, specific, and tied to one workflow.

Do not invite the whole company. Invite the workflow owner and the people who carry the consequence if the workflow goes wrong. Depending on the use case, that may include the CFO, CIO, CISO, Head of Support, Head of Marketing, or another operator with direct ownership.

A useful meeting usually takes twenty to thirty minutes.

The goal is not to approve AI in general.

The goal is to leave the room with one written decision:

What may AI do, under what conditions, with what evidence, and when must a human take over?

Use this sequence.

First, name the workflow in one sentence.

Not "use AI in support."

Say: "Use AI to summarize inbound support tickets and recommend whether they are routine, urgent, security-sensitive, or escalation-required."

Second, name the decision.

If the team cannot name the decision, the use case is still too vague.

In this example, the decision is:

Should this ticket be routed normally, reviewed by a technician, escalated immediately, or stopped until missing information is provided?

Third, identify the owner.

For this workflow, the Head of Support may own service quality. The CIO may own the system and integration rules. The CISO may own security escalation criteria. The CFO may care whether the workflow really lowers cost or only shifts labor to senior staff. If the workflow touches customer promises or customer-facing follow-up, the Head of Marketing or customer communications owner may also need to define what AI is not allowed to send.

Fourth, decide AI's role.

Can AI assist by summarizing the ticket and extracting missing fields?

Can it recommend severity?

Can it act by routing only a narrow class of routine cases?

Must it escalate when security language, executive users, multi-user outages, or missing client context appear?

Must it stop when required evidence is missing or the case touches regulated data?

This is the point of the meeting.

The team is not trying to admire the tool.

It is trying to write the boundary.

A practical boundary discussion sounds like this:

The Head of Support says, "AI may summarize every ticket. It may recommend category and priority."

The CISO says, "AI may not downgrade tickets that mention suspicious login behavior, terminated users, unusual access, endpoint protection alerts, or privileged accounts."

The CIO says, "AI may not route a ticket automatically unless required fields are present and the integration shows the affected system clearly."

The CFO says, "Do not claim labor savings unless we measure reopen rate, senior-review burden, and escalation quality after deployment."

The Head of Marketing says, "If the workflow later feeds customer updates, AI may not send external language without approved templates and ownership."

Now the meeting is useful.

The boundary begins to take shape.

Here is the working output the team should leave with:

Decision: classify and route inbound tickets.

AI may assist by summarizing ticket history, extracting affected systems, identifying missing information, and preparing a routing recommendation.

AI may recommend routine routing when the issue matches approved low-risk categories and the required context is complete.

AI may act only on a narrow set of low-risk requests such as standard password-reset or access-restoration tickets that do not involve privileged users, terminated users, unusual login patterns, security alerts, contract exceptions, or executive accounts.

AI must escalate when sensitive systems, suspicious identity activity, repeated failed access, executive users, multi-user impact, missing context, or security-sensitive language appears.

AI must stop when the request falls outside approved categories or required data is missing.

Human owner: Head of Support.

Control owners: CIO for system controls, CISO for escalation triggers, CFO for economic proof.

Success metric: lower low-risk triage time without increasing reopen rate, security misses, senior-review burden, or customer dissatisfaction.

This is what most organizations skip.

They discuss AI capability and never write the operating rule.

If the team has time for only one more step, add two columns:

What evidence must AI show?

What would make this unsafe?

Those two questions often reveal the real boundary faster than a long debate.

Mini-Template: The 20-Minute Boundary Meeting

Workflow:

____

Decision:

____

AI may assist by:

____

AI may recommend when:

____

AI may act only when:

____

AI must escalate when:

____

AI must stop when:

____

Human owner:

____

Control owners:

____

Success metric:

____

If the team cannot fill these blanks clearly, the use case is not ready.

A blurry boundary is not a flexible boundary.

It is an undiscovered risk.

The best Decision Boundary meetings are not theoretical.

They are operational.

They name the workflow, the decision, the owner, the evidence, the triggers, and the stop conditions.

That is how a CIO gets clarity.

That is how a CISO gets protection.

That is how a CFO gets honest economics.

That is how a Head of Support gets cleaner operations.

That is how a Head of Marketing avoids AI output that creates customer confusion or trust damage.

That is how AI becomes manageable.

Not through slogans.

Through a written boundary the team can actually use.

Chapter 12 will build on this by showing how to design workflows around the four practical AI roles: assist, recommend, act, and escalate.

Decision Architect's Field Notes

What to Do Next

Pick one AI-supported decision and complete the boundary template.

Then test it against ten real cases. Include easy cases, messy cases, and high-risk cases.

If AI's role stays clear, the boundary is useful.

If the role becomes confusing, narrow the use case or add escalation triggers.

Common Traps to Avoid

Do not define AI's role for the whole department. Define it for one decision at a time.

Do not let AI act on judgment-based decisions without strong human ownership.

Do not use "human in the loop" as a substitute for role, evidence, and escalation rules.

Do not let low-risk automation drift into high-risk decision influence.

Do not scale until ordinary users understand the boundary.

Boardroom Question

Which AI decisions have a written boundary showing what AI may do, what humans own, what evidence is required, and when the system must escalate or stop?

Industry Translation

In MSPs, the boundary protects escalation quality and client trust.

In cybersecurity, it protects response ownership and incident discipline.

In finance, it protects payment control and audit readiness.

In marketing and GTM, it protects proof, claims, and buyer trust.

In operations, it protects throughput without hiding exceptions.

Implementation Law

Every AI action without a defined boundary is a liability, not a feature.

Chapter 12 - Design: Assist, Recommend, Act, or Escalate

How to Build AI Into the Workflow Without Losing Control

Once the Decision Boundary is defined, the next mistake is poor workflow design.

A team may agree that AI should only recommend, but the screen makes the recommendation look like an instruction. A manager may agree that AI should escalate risk, but the escalation appears as a small note buried under the summary. A user may understand that AI is only assisting, but the workflow makes the AI output look complete, final, and safe.

That is how good policy becomes weak implementation.

The blind spot is this:

Organizations define AI's role in theory but fail to design the workflow so people behave correctly in practice.

This is where many AI projects quietly lose control. The organization says the right words. "Human in the loop." "AI-assisted." "Reviewed by staff." "Subject to approval." But the actual workflow tells a different story.

The button says Approve.

The AI text says Recommended.

The employee is rushed.

The evidence is hidden.

The exception signal is hard to see.

The system logs the final action but not the reasoning.

Then leadership is surprised when people overtrust the output.

That is not a user problem.

That is a design problem.

Good AI workflow design makes the safe action the easy action.

AI Roles Must Be Designed Into the Work

Chapter 11 defined the core roles: assist, recommend, act, escalate, and stop. Chapter 12 turns those roles into workflow design.

If AI assists, the workflow should help the human see better. The output should not pretend to be a decision. It should organize information, show sources, identify missing data, and make review easier.

If AI recommends, the workflow should make review unavoidable before the recommendation changes the business process. A recommendation should show the reason, the supporting evidence, the uncertainty, and the escalation triggers.

If AI acts, the action must be narrow, low risk, logged, monitored, and reversible when possible. AI should act only when rules are clear and exceptions are already defined.

If AI escalates, escalation must be visible, fast, and routed to the right owner. An escalation hidden in a note is not a real escalation.

If AI must stop, the workflow should block the next step until a human owner reviews the issue.

This sounds simple. It is not.

Many AI workflows fail because they give AI a safe role in policy but an unsafe role in practice.

For example, a finance team may say AI only "suggests" routine invoice status. But if the system displays a green status label, places the item inside the normal approval queue, and does not show exception evidence clearly, users may treat the suggestion as approval.

A cybersecurity team may say AI only "summarizes" alerts. But if the summary places "likely low priority" at the top and hides privileged-user context at the bottom, the workflow nudges analysts toward underreaction.

A marketing team may say AI only "drafts" campaign language. But if the draft is placed directly into the publishing workflow without proof review, the draft becomes operationally close to final.

The design teaches behavior.

If the design encourages overtrust, training will not fully fix it.

The Four Design Controls

A practical AI workflow needs four controls.

1. Label the Output Clearly

AI output should be labeled by role.

A draft should look like a draft.

A recommendation should look like a recommendation.

An evidence summary should look like an evidence summary.

An approved action should look different from an AI suggestion.

Do not let every AI output appear in the same polished format. Polished language creates psychological authority. If the output is only a draft, the interface and workflow should make that obvious.

Good labels include:

Draft for Review
Recommendation — Human Approval Required
Evidence Summary
Exception Detected
Escalation Required
Blocked — Missing Required Evidence

Bad labels include vague phrases such as:

AI Complete
Ready
Optimized
Approved by AI
Low Risk without explanation

The label should match the business meaning.

2. Show the Reason

A recommendation without visible reasoning creates two bad behaviors.

Some users overtrust it.

Others reject it because they cannot see why it was made.

Neither is ideal.

The workflow should show why AI recommended something in plain business language.

For a ticket, the reason may be:

"Recommended routine routing because the issue matches approved low-risk access patterns, no executive user is involved, no security-sensitive language appears, and client context is complete."

For an invoice, the reason may be:

"Recommended exception review because payment details changed and purchase order match is incomplete."

For a campaign claim, the reason may be:

"Review required because the draft includes a performance claim without approved proof."

This is not technical explainability for machine learning researchers.

This is business explainability for operators.

The user must be able to understand why the workflow is moving.

3. Separate Routine From Exception

Routine work and exception work should not live in the same lane.

If users must search for risk, risk will be missed.

AI should help separate ordinary flow from exception flow. That is one of its best uses.

Routine work can move faster when evidence is complete, risk is low, and rules are clear.

Exception work should rise to the surface when information is missing, risk increases, rules conflict, or ownership is unclear.

In finance, changed bank details should not sit quietly inside routine invoice review.

In support, a VIP customer or multi-user outage should not be hidden inside a normal category.

In cybersecurity, privileged-user activity should not be treated as a footnote.

In marketing, unsupported claims should not enter final approval as ordinary copy.

A good workflow does not ask busy humans to notice every risk manually. It designs risk visibility into the path.

4. Log Important Actions

If AI influences a meaningful decision, the organization should preserve the record.

The log does not need to be complicated, but it should answer practical questions:

What did AI produce?

What evidence did it use?

Who reviewed it?

What changed?

What decision was made?

Was anything escalated?

Why did the workflow proceed?

This matters for quality, audit, compliance, training, vendor evaluation, and future improvement.

A workflow that cannot explain itself later is not production-ready for important decisions.

Design for Ordinary Users, Not Power Users

Many AI pilots work because one strong user knows how to handle the tool.

That is not enough.

Production workflows must work for ordinary users on ordinary days under ordinary pressure.

People will be busy. They will skim. They will trust green labels. They will miss small warnings. They will choose the faster path if the safer path is harder. They will assume the system was designed correctly.

This is why workflow design matters more than training alone.

Training tells people what they should do.

Workflow design makes the correct action easier to do.

If escalation takes five clicks and approval takes one click, the system is biased toward approval.

If evidence is hidden behind a tab, people will skip it.

If uncertainty appears in technical language, people will ignore it.

If AI output looks finished, people will treat it as finished.

A strong design should pass the ordinary-user test:

Would a trained but busy employee understand what AI is doing, what they still own, what evidence matters, and when they must escalate?

If not, the workflow is not ready.

Modeled Example: The Invoice Screen That Looked Too Safe

The following is a modeled example for planning purposes, not an audited client result.

A finance team uses AI to help classify invoices.

The AI extracts vendor name, invoice amount, purchase order number, payment terms, and due date. It compares the fields against approved records and recommends one of three statuses: routine, review, or exception.

During testing, the tool appears accurate.

But during workflow review, the Decision Architect notices a design problem.

The AI recommendation appears as a large green label:

Routine

Below the label, in smaller text, the system notes:

"Banking details changed since last payment."

The finance analyst sees the green label first. The item appears inside the routine queue. The changed-bank-detail warning is technically visible, but operationally weak.

This is poor design.

The system is saying two different things: routine and risky.

The redesign is simple but powerful.

The label changes to:

Exception Detected — Payment Detail Change

The invoice is removed from the routine queue.

The analyst must complete a verification step before approval.

The system records the exception trigger, reviewer, verification result, approver, and decision time.

AI still helps. It extracts fields, compares records, and identifies the exception faster.

But the workflow no longer lets a risky item travel under a routine label.

This is the difference between AI output and AI implementation.

The AI result did not need more intelligence.

The workflow needed better design.

The Real Lesson

AI workflow design is where strategy becomes behavior.

A policy can say AI should assist.

A workflow can make it look like AI approved.

A governance document can say escalation is required.

A screen can hide the escalation signal.

A training session can tell employees to review output carefully.

A rushed workflow can make careful review unlikely.

This is why design matters.

Do not blame users first.

Inspect the workflow.

Does the output label match the AI role?

Is the evidence visible?

Are exceptions surfaced?

Is escalation easier than risky approval?

Are important actions logged?

Does the design make the safe action the easy action?

If the answer is no, the AI project is not ready to scale.

Decision Architect's Field Notes

What to Do Next

Choose one AI workflow and inspect it from the user's point of view.

Do not review the policy. Review the actual screen, form, message, approval path, or handoff.

Ask:

What does the user see first?

Does AI output look like a draft, recommendation, or final decision?

Is the reason visible?

Is missing information visible?

Are exceptions separated from routine cases?

Is escalation obvious?

Is approval too easy?

Is the action logged?

Then test the workflow with ordinary users, not only power users.

Give them real cases: easy cases, messy cases, and risky cases. Watch what they do. If they overtrust the AI, miss exceptions, or struggle to explain the decision, redesign the workflow.

Common Traps to Avoid

Do not rely on training to compensate for poor design.

Do not let AI recommendations look like approvals.

Do not hide uncertainty or exceptions in small print.

Do not make escalation harder than approval.

Do not allow AI actions without logs.

Do not assume power-user behavior will repeat across ordinary users.

Do not let routine and high-risk cases share the same visual path.

Boardroom Question

Are our AI workflows designed so employees naturally review, escalate, and document correctly — or are we depending on memory, caution, and hope?

Industry Translation

In finance, workflow design protects payment approvals, exception review, and audit readiness.

In MSP and IT services, it protects escalation quality, client context, and service reliability.

In cybersecurity, it protects alert severity, analyst judgment, and response ownership.

In marketing and GTM, it protects proof, claims, brand trust, and buyer relevance.

In healthcare administration, it protects role boundaries, privacy, and patient-facing communication.

Implementation Law

AI workflow design should make the safe action the easy action.

Chapter 13 - Pilot and Prove: Reality Tests, Evidence Packs, and Real ROI

How to Test AI Without Fooling Yourself

A pilot is not proof because people liked it.

A pilot is not proof because the output looked good.

A pilot is not proof because the vendor demo was impressive.

A pilot becomes useful when it produces evidence strong enough to support a decision.

That decision may be scale.

It may be redesign.

It may be continue testing with a specific unanswered question.

It may be stop.

All four outcomes are legitimate.

The blind spot is this:

Organizations run AI pilots to create momentum instead of running them to answer specific business questions.

That is why so many pilots become confusing. The team tests a tool, likes the output, collects positive comments, shows a few examples, and calls the result promising.

Promising is not enough.

A serious pilot should answer one question:

Does this AI-assisted workflow improve the business after review, correction, exceptions, risk, and cost are counted?

If the pilot cannot answer that question, it may still be interesting. It may still teach something. But it has not yet proven implementation value.

Start With the Question, Not the Tool

A good pilot begins before the first AI output is generated.

It begins with a clear test question.

Weak pilot question:

"Can AI help our support team?"

Better pilot question:

"Can AI reduce low-risk ticket triage time without increasing reopen rate, escalation errors, or senior technician review burden?"

Weak pilot question:

"Can AI improve marketing?"

Better pilot question:

"Can AI reduce campaign brief preparation time while improving sales acceptance and reducing unsupported claims?"

Weak pilot question:

"Can AI help finance process invoices?"

Better pilot question:

"Can AI reduce routine invoice review time while improving exception visibility and preserving audit evidence?"

The sharper question creates the sharper pilot.

It defines the workflow.

It defines the decision.

It defines the risk.

It defines what evidence matters.

A pilot without a clear question becomes a performance.

A pilot with a clear question becomes a test.

The Evidence Pack

Every serious AI pilot should produce an Evidence Pack.

The Evidence Pack is not a long consultant report. It is a short proof file that helps leaders decide what to do next.

It should include:

Workflow: What process is being tested?

Decision: What decision does AI support?

Baseline: How does the workflow perform today?

AI role: Does AI assist, recommend, act, escalate, or stop?

Boundary: What is AI allowed to do, and what is it not allowed to do?

Risk level: Is this low, medium, or high risk?

Evidence required: What must AI show or preserve?

Metrics: What proves improvement?

Rework: What verification, correction, and exception handling remain?

Cost: What do tool usage, training, integration, monitoring, review, and governance cost?

Recommendation: Scale, redesign, continue testing, or stop?

Keep it practical. One or two pages may be enough.

The point is not paperwork.

The point is to prevent self-deception.

An Evidence Pack forces the team to separate what felt useful from what actually improved.

Define the Baseline Before the Pilot

Many AI pilots fail because the team does not know the starting point.

They test AI and then try to estimate improvement afterward.

That creates weak evidence.

Before the pilot begins, measure the baseline.

How long does the workflow take today?

How often do errors occur?

How often do cases reopen?

How much review is required?

How many exceptions occur?

Who handles them?

What is the cost per completed unit?

What is the customer impact?

What is the current risk?

The baseline does not need to be perfect, but it must be honest.

A useful baseline can begin with a small sample. Twenty-five real cases can reveal more than a large meeting. Fifty cases may be better. One hundred may be useful for high-volume workflows.

The key is to use real work, not artificial examples.

Clean examples create clean pilots.

Messy examples create useful pilots.

Test Three Kinds of Cases

A serious AI pilot should test three kinds of cases.

First, test routine cases.

These show whether AI can help with normal workflow.

Second, test messy cases.

These show whether AI handles missing information, ambiguous context, incomplete records, unusual wording, or inconsistent source data.

Third, test high-risk or edge cases.

These show whether AI knows when to escalate or stop.

Many pilots test only routine cases because routine cases make the tool look good.

That is not enough.

The business does not get hurt most by routine cases.

It gets hurt by exceptions that look routine until someone looks closer.

A support ticket that says "login issue" may involve identity compromise.

An invoice that looks routine may include changed bank details.

A marketing claim that sounds polished may lack proof.

A security alert that looks familiar may involve a privileged user.

A pilot that cannot detect the difference between routine and risky is not ready to scale.

Success Metrics and Stop Conditions

Before the pilot begins, define success.

Success cannot be "users liked it."

User enthusiasm is useful, but it is not proof.

Better success metrics include:

Reduced cycle time.

Lower review burden.

Fewer errors.

Better escalation accuracy.

Lower cost per completed unit.

Reduced reopen rate.

Higher sales acceptance.

Improved response time.

Reduced exception delay.

Stronger audit evidence.

Improved customer satisfaction.

Better use of expert time.

Also define stop conditions.

Stop or redesign if review burden erases the gain.

Stop if risk cannot be bounded.

Stop if data quality is too weak.

Stop if ordinary users cannot repeat the result.

Stop if the workflow only works when a power user supervises it.

Stop if the AI output cannot preserve enough evidence.

Stop if the project cannot explain its financial path.

Stop conditions are not negative.

They protect the organization.

They also make the pilot more honest.

If the team knows what failure looks like before testing, it is less likely to rationalize weak results afterward.

Real ROI Means Net Value, Not Gross Speed

The most common AI pilot mistake is fake ROI.

The team says AI saved time.

Then it multiplies saved minutes by wages and calls the result savings.

That may be valid in some situations. But not automatically.

The better question is:

What changed because time was saved?

Did cost go down?

Did capacity increase?

Did revenue improve?

Did margin improve?

Did risk decrease?

Did quality improve?

Did expert review burden fall?

If the answer is unclear, the ROI claim is premature.

A pilot should calculate net value, not gross speed.

That means counting:

AI-assisted time.

Verification time.

Correction time.

Exception handling.

Human review.

Tool cost.

Usage cost.

Integration.

Training.

Monitoring.

Governance.

The first output is not the finished economics.

The trusted workflow is the economics.

Modeled Example: The Sales Follow-Up Pilot

The following is a modeled example for planning purposes, not an audited client result.

A B2B sales team tests AI for post-discovery follow-up.

Before AI, reps take about forty minutes to prepare a quality follow-up after a discovery call. The follow-up must reflect buyer pain points, objections, agreed next steps, product fit, and approved proof.

The first AI pilot generates polished emails in five minutes.

The team is excited.

The early claim is:

"AI saves thirty-five minutes per follow-up."

Then the sales manager reviews the full workflow.

Some drafts are useful. Others sound generic. A few include unsupported claims. Some miss important objections. Some overstate product fit. Reps still spend time editing.

The team adjusts the pilot.

AI may draft only from approved call notes, approved proof points, product constraints, and stated next steps.

AI must identify missing information.

AI must flag unsupported claims.

The account owner must review before sending.

The revised measurement includes:

Draft time.

Review time.

Manager rewrite burden.

Buyer response.

Meeting conversion.

Unsupported claim rate.

Sales acceptance.

After testing real cases, the team finds that AI does not save thirty-five minutes per follow-up. It saves about twelve to eighteen minutes on usable follow-ups while improving consistency when inputs are strong.

That is still valuable.

But the business case is now honest.

The project does not scale as "AI writes sales emails."

It scales as:

"AI prepares buyer-specific follow-up drafts from approved discovery evidence, reducing rep preparation time while protecting proof and message quality."

That is a much stronger implementation.

The Real Lesson

A good pilot should make the next decision easier.

It should not create fog.

The purpose of a pilot is not to impress leadership.

It is not to justify a tool already purchased.

It is not to create a success story for a slide.

The purpose of a pilot is to answer a business question with enough evidence to decide what happens next.

Scale.

Redesign.

Continue testing with a specific question.

Stop.

If a pilot does not produce one of those decisions, it is unfinished.

A pilot that ends with "this was interesting" may have created learning.

A pilot that ends with "we should explore more" may be avoiding judgment.

A pilot that ends with "scale this defined workflow under these boundaries because the evidence supports it" is implementation discipline.

That is the standard.

Decision Architect's Field Notes

What to Do Next

For the next AI pilot, write the Evidence Pack before testing.

Begin with one clear pilot question:

Does this AI-assisted workflow improve ___________ after review, correction, exceptions, risk, and cost are counted?

Then define the baseline, AI role, decision boundary, risk level, evidence requirements, success metrics, and stop conditions.

Use real cases. Include routine cases, messy cases, and edge cases.

After the pilot, force one decision:

Scale.

Redesign.

Continue testing with one specific unanswered question.

Stop.

Do not let the pilot drift.

Common Traps to Avoid

Do not run pilots without a baseline.

Do not test only clean examples.

Do not treat user enthusiasm as ROI.

Do not ignore review, correction, exception handling, or senior oversight.

Do not let vendors define success for you.

Do not multiply saved minutes by wages unless the saved time creates real economic change.

Do not continue testing unless the next test answers a specific question.

Boardroom Question

Which AI pilots have produced enough evidence to justify scale, and which are still only interesting experiments?

Industry Translation

In MSPs, pilots should measure triage quality, reopen rate, escalation accuracy, and technician review burden.

In cybersecurity, pilots should measure evidence preparation, severity accuracy, analyst workload, and escalation discipline.

In finance, pilots should separate routine processing from exceptions and high-risk approvals.

In marketing and GTM, pilots should measure sales acceptance, proof quality, buyer relevance, and conversion signals.

In operations, pilots should measure completed work, handoff quality, exception handling, and downstream rework.

Implementation Law

A pilot is valuable only when it produces evidence for a decision.

Chapter 14 - Scale or Stop: The Discipline of Implementation

Why Stopping Weak AI Projects Protects Strong Ones

The pilot worked well enough to continue.

That was the problem.

It did not fail. It did not prove scale. It did not produce a clean business case. It simply stayed alive.

A few people liked it. The vendor kept supporting it. Managers mentioned it in updates. Nobody wanted to stop it because stopping sounded negative.

Six months later, the project had consumed meetings, licenses, attention, and credibility without changing the business.

This is one of the quietest ways AI strategy fails.

Not through disaster.

Through drift.

The blind spot is this:

Organizations know how to start AI projects but not how to stop weak ones.

They launch pilots. They approve tools. They encourage experimentation. They collect stories. They create dashboards. But they do not build the discipline to decide which projects deserve production and which should end.

Without that discipline, the AI portfolio becomes cluttered.

Some projects are useful.

Some are weak.

Some are risky.

Some are redundant.

Some are nobody's responsibility anymore.

All of them consume attention.

That is why scale-or-stop discipline matters.

What Scale-or-Stop Discipline Means

Scale-or-stop discipline is the practice of deciding whether an AI initiative deserves expansion, redesign, continued testing, or termination.

It is not anti-innovation.

It is how innovation becomes manageable.

A serious organization does not treat every AI pilot as a future production system. Most pilots should not scale. Some should teach. Some should be redesigned. Some should reveal that the workflow is not ready. Some should show that the value is too small.

That is normal.

The danger is pretending every pilot deserves more time.

A pilot should move toward one of four decisions.

Scale when the evidence is strong, the boundary is clear, the economics make sense, and the production path is credible.

Redesign when the opportunity is real but the workflow, data, role, risk control, or measurement approach is wrong.

Continue testing only when there is a specific unanswered question.

Stop when the value is weak, the risk is too high, the data is not ready, the cost does not scale, or the workflow should be fixed before AI enters.

The strongest AI organizations will not be the ones with the most pilots.

They will be the ones with the clearest decisions.

The Six Conditions for Scale

A serious scale decision should require six conditions.

1. Workflow Fit

The workflow must be specific enough to manage.

"Use AI in operations" is not a workflow.

"Use AI to prepare exception packets for delayed supplier shipments" is closer.

A project should not scale if the workflow is still vague.

2. Decision Fit

The AI-supported decision must be named.

Does AI help decide what to route, approve, escalate, draft, investigate, prioritize, send, stop, or review?

If no decision can be named, the use case is probably activity, not implementation.

3. Boundary Fit

The Decision Boundary must be written.

What can AI assist with?

What can it recommend?

Where may it act?

When must it escalate?

When must it stop?

If ordinary users cannot explain the boundary, the project is not ready for production.

4. Evidence and Economics Fit

The pilot must show improvement after review, correction, exception handling, risk, and cost are counted.

Gross speed is not enough.

A project that saves frontline time but increases senior review may still be weak. A project that produces more output but does not improve outcomes may not deserve scale.

5. Risk Fit

The AI role must match the risk level.

Low-risk drafting can move faster.

Medium-risk recommendations need review.

High-risk decisions involving money, security, compliance, healthcare administration, legal exposure, customer commitments, or employee impact need stronger ownership and auditability.

Risk does not always block AI.

It narrows AI's role.

6. Production Fit

The workflow must survive ordinary users, real data, expected volume, integration needs, monitoring, training, support burden, vendor reliability, and cost behavior.

A project that works only with a power user is not production-ready.

A project that works only on clean data is not production-ready.

A project that nobody owns is not production-ready.

These six conditions protect scale from wishful thinking.

Why Stopping Is a Strength

Stopping a weak AI project feels uncomfortable because it can look like failure.

It is not.

Stopping is intelligent capital protection.

It protects money, time, trust, attention, and credibility. It also protects strong projects from being crowded out by weak ones.

A project may need to stop because the data is not ready.

That is useful knowledge.

A project may need to stop because the review burden erases the gain.

That is useful knowledge.

A project may need to stop because risk cannot be controlled.

That is useful knowledge.

A project may need to stop because the workflow is too vague.

That is useful knowledge.

A project may need to stop because the value is real but too small to justify production.

That is useful knowledge.

Stopping does not mean AI failed.

It means the organization learned before spending more.

That is mature implementation.

The worst outcome is not a stopped project.

The worst outcome is a weak project that survives because nobody wants to make a decision.

Modeled Example: The Reporting Pilot That Needed to Stop

The following is a modeled example for planning purposes, not an audited client result.

A mid-market company tests AI for weekly executive reporting.

Before AI, managers spend about twelve hours collecting updates, summarizing activity, preparing slides, and answering leadership questions.

The AI pilot pulls data from project tools, CRM notes, support tickets, meeting transcripts, and finance summaries. It creates a polished weekly report.

The first output looks impressive.

The formatting is clean. The summaries are readable. The executive team likes the speed.

Then the CEO asks:

"What should I pay attention to?"

The report does not answer well.

It summarizes activity but does not separate material risk from ordinary movement. It repeats optimistic manager language without challenge. It treats minor tasks and serious blockers with similar weight. It misses weak signals buried in support tickets. Finance does not fully trust some numbers. Operations says some status labels mean different things across teams.

The AI made the report look better.

It did not make the management system better.

The team tries redesign.

AI will no longer produce the final executive report. It will prepare evidence packets by department: metric changes, open risks, overdue decisions, customer-impacting issues, resource constraints, unresolved escalations, confidence level, and missing updates.

That is a better design.

But then the real problem appears.

The source systems are inconsistent. Managers define "on track" differently. Key metrics are not updated reliably. Critical context lives in informal conversations. Some customer risks are not entered anywhere.

AI cannot fix a management reporting system that leadership has not standardized.

The scale decision is stop.

Not forever.

For now.

The company redirects effort to define reporting standards, metric ownership, escalation categories, and decision rules.

AI may return later as an evidence-preparation layer.

Stopping protects the company from scaling a polished reporting machine that would create false confidence.

This is exactly what scale-or-stop discipline is for.

The Portfolio View

Scale-or-stop discipline becomes even more important when an organization has many AI activities.

One pilot may not seem expensive.

Twenty weak pilots are expensive.

They consume meetings, licenses, user attention, vendor conversations, IT review, security review, finance review, compliance review, and executive patience.

This is how AI clutter forms.

A practical AI portfolio should group projects into four categories:

Scale candidates have evidence, economics, boundaries, owners, and production readiness.

Redesign candidates have real opportunity but need workflow, data, boundary, risk, or measurement repair.

Learning pilots are still answering a specific question.

Stop candidates no longer justify attention.

This view helps leaders manage AI like an operating portfolio, not a collection of experiments.

A portfolio review should ask:

Which projects are creating measurable value?

Which projects are creating learning?

Which projects are creating risk?

Which projects are duplicative?

Which projects have no owner?

Which projects should stop this month?

That last question should be normal.

If nothing ever stops, the AI portfolio is not being managed.

How to Make the Scale Decision

At the end of every pilot, require a short scale-or-stop review.

Do not make it theatrical.

Make it operational.

The review should answer:

What workflow was tested?

What decision did AI support?

What baseline was used?

What changed?

What did review and correction cost?

What exceptions appeared?

What risk was created or reduced?

What evidence supports the result?

What production cost will appear at scale?

Who owns the outcome?

What is the recommendation?

Then choose one of four decisions:

Scale.

Redesign.

Continue testing with one specific question.

Stop.

The phrase "continue testing" must be controlled. It should not mean "we are not ready to decide."

It should mean:

"We need to answer this specific question next."

For example:

Can ordinary users repeat the result?

Can exception handling be reduced?

Can the workflow work with live data?

Can the tool preserve enough evidence?

Can cost remain acceptable at production volume?

If there is no specific question, continued testing is drift.

The Real Lesson

AI implementation requires courage in both directions.

It takes courage to scale a strong project.

It also takes courage to stop a weak one.

Many organizations are comfortable starting. Fewer are disciplined enough to decide.

That is why AI portfolios become crowded with half-alive pilots.

A serious implementation culture treats stopping as part of strategy.

Stopping weak projects protects strong ones.

Stopping vague projects protects clarity.

Stopping risky projects protects trust.

Stopping low-value projects protects capital.

Stopping drift protects credibility.

The goal is not to reduce AI ambition.

The goal is to make AI ambition earn its place inside the business.

When projects must prove workflow fit, decision fit, boundary fit, evidence and economics fit, risk fit, and production fit, scale becomes credible.

That is how AI moves from experimentation to operating discipline.

Decision Architect's Field Notes

What to Do Next

Create a scale-or-stop review for every active AI pilot.

For each project, assign one decision:

Scale.

Redesign.

Continue testing with one specific question.

Stop.

Then write one sentence explaining why.

Do not allow vague continuation.

If the team cannot explain the next decision, stop the drift and return to the Evidence Pack.

Common Traps to Avoid

Do not keep pilots alive because they were once exciting.

Do not scale without a named workflow, decision, owner, boundary, and evidence.

Do not treat "continue testing" as a way to avoid judgment.

Do not treat stopping as embarrassment.

Do not let weak projects consume the attention needed by stronger ones.

Do not let vendors define whether a project deserves production.

Do not scale a workflow that ordinary users cannot operate safely.

Boardroom Question

Which AI projects should scale, which should be redesigned, and which should stop before they consume more capital, trust, and management attention?

Industry Translation

In MSP and IT services, scale-or-stop discipline protects technician capacity, escalation quality, and client trust.

In cybersecurity, it prevents useful evidence tools from being overextended into unsafe response automation.

In marketing and GTM, it stops content-volume experiments that do not improve buyer relevance or pipeline quality.

In finance, it prevents ROI overclaims and protects payment, audit, and exception controls.

In operations, it stops workflow automation that makes handoffs faster but downstream quality worse.

Implementation Law

Stopping a weak AI project is not failure. It is intelligent capital protection.

Part IV - Enterprise System Playbooks

Chapter 15 - The Revenue Engine

Sales, Marketing, GTM, and Customer Success

Revenue teams are often the first to adopt AI because the use cases look obvious.

Write more emails. Create more campaigns. Summarize sales calls. Build account plans. Draft proposals. Generate social posts. Personalize outreach. Analyze customer feedback. Predict churn. Prepare renewal messages.

The surface opportunity is real.

But revenue is also one of the easiest places to confuse AI activity with business impact.

The marketing team may produce more content without improving buyer trust. Sales may send more messages without improving meeting quality. Customer success may summarize more account notes without reducing churn. Leadership may see dashboards full of AI usage but no meaningful change in pipeline, win rate, retention, margin, or customer confidence.

The blind spot is this:

Revenue AI often increases communication volume before it improves buyer decisions.

That is dangerous because revenue is not created by output volume. Revenue is created when the right buyer, at the right moment, receives enough credible information to take the next step.

AI can help that process. But only if it is designed around the buyer decision, not around internal content production.

The Revenue Engine Is a Decision System

Sales, marketing, GTM, and customer success are not just communication functions.

They are decision systems.

Marketing helps the buyer decide whether the company is relevant.

Sales helps the buyer decide whether the solution is credible.

Customer success helps the customer decide whether the relationship is still valuable.

GTM leadership decides where to focus resources, which segments matter, which messages deserve investment, which accounts deserve attention, and which opportunities are real.

AI should support these decisions.

It should not simply multiply content.

In a revenue engine, AI can assist with research, call summaries, account briefs, campaign planning, objection analysis, customer health signals, proposal drafts, and renewal preparation. But every AI-supported output should connect to a decision:

Which buyer segment are we targeting?

What problem matters most to this buyer?

What proof do we have?

What claim can we honestly make?

What objection must we address?

What next step should the buyer take?

What account needs intervention?

What customer risk signal requires action?

When AI is not tied to these questions, it becomes a volume machine.

Volume without relevance weakens revenue quality.

Where AI Helps the Revenue Engine

AI is useful in revenue work when it reduces friction around insight, preparation, and follow-through.

In marketing, AI can turn approved positioning, customer objections, sales-call notes, case evidence, and product limits into campaign briefs. It can identify weak claims, missing proof, repeated language, and unclear calls to action.

In sales, AI can prepare account research, summarize discovery calls, draft follow-up messages, identify buyer concerns, compare stakeholder priorities, and prepare proposal outlines.

In customer success, AI can summarize account history, detect recurring issues, organize renewal risks, prepare business review notes, and identify patterns across support tickets, usage data, and customer feedback.

In GTM strategy, AI can help compare segments, analyze win-loss notes, cluster objections, and surface patterns that are too scattered for manual review.

But the decision boundary must stay clear.

AI may draft. Humans own claims.

AI may summarize. Humans own interpretation.

AI may recommend next steps. Account owners own judgment.

AI may detect churn signals. Customer success leaders own intervention strategy.

AI may prepare campaign options. Marketing leaders own positioning.

The more customer-facing or revenue-sensitive the output, the more important the review standard becomes.

A Practical Revenue AI Workflow

A strong revenue use case is not "use AI to write more sales emails."

A stronger use case is:

Use AI to convert approved discovery notes, buyer pain points, objections, account context, and proof points into a reviewed follow-up message that supports a specific buyer decision.

That workflow has structure.

The trigger is a completed discovery call.

The actors are the sales rep, manager if needed, and AI assistant.

The decision is: what should the buyer receive next to move the opportunity forward responsibly?

The required evidence includes call notes, buyer priorities, stated objections, product fit, approved proof, pricing constraints, and next-step agreement.

AI's role is to assist and recommend. It may draft the follow-up and suggest the likely buyer concern. It should not invent ROI, promise outcomes, create fake case studies, or change pricing.

The human owner is the account owner.

The success measures are follow-up speed, message quality, meeting progression, buyer response, opportunity stage movement, and reduction in manager rewrite burden.

This is practical AI.

It does not ask AI to "sell."

It asks AI to help the salesperson prepare a better buyer-specific decision support message.

That distinction protects trust.

Modeled Example: The Marketing Team That Produced More and Moved Less

The following is a modeled example for planning purposes, not an audited client result.

A B2B company adopts AI to increase campaign output.

Before AI, the team produces six campaign assets per month.

After AI, it produces eighteen.

Leadership likes the activity. Website traffic rises slightly. Social posting becomes consistent. Email volume increases.

But sales complains that the campaigns sound generic. Legal flags unsupported claims. The CEO says the messaging could belong to any competitor. Pipeline quality does not improve.

The first AI implementation solved the wrong problem.

The bottleneck was not content production.

The bottleneck was buyer relevance and proof quality.

The company redesigns the workflow.

AI no longer begins with "write a campaign."

It begins with a campaign evidence pack: target segment, buyer pain, approved claims, proof points, objections, competitor pressure, sales notes, customer language, and compliance constraints.

AI drafts a campaign brief, not a final campaign.

The marketing owner reviews proof strength. Sales reviews buyer relevance. Legal reviews only claims that cross a risk threshold. AI flags claims without evidence.

The output volume may decrease.

The revenue quality improves.

The team now measures sales acceptance, campaign readiness, rewrite burden, claim defects, qualified response, and opportunity influence.

That is the right lesson for revenue AI.

More output is not the win.

Better buyer movement is the win.

Implementation Advice for Revenue Teams

Start with one revenue decision, not the whole funnel.

Good candidates include post-discovery follow-up, campaign brief creation, renewal risk summaries, sales-call objection extraction, proposal preparation, account research, or customer health review.

Require approved inputs. Revenue AI becomes dangerous when it invents proof. Give it the facts it is allowed to use.

Separate internal drafts from customer-facing communication. AI can create first drafts quickly, but anything that touches a buyer should pass through a human owner.

Measure quality, not just volume. Track sales acceptance, response quality, meeting conversion, campaign readiness, rewrite burden, churn-risk detection, renewal movement, and customer trust signals.

Build stop rules. AI should stop or escalate when claims involve regulated industries, pricing promises, customer results, legal commitments, competitive comparisons, security guarantees, or financial outcomes.

Failure Hotspot: AI Outreach That Damages Buyer Trust

One of the fastest ways to weaken a revenue engine is to let AI create the appearance of personalization without the substance of relevance.

A team loads account lists into a sales engagement platform, asks AI to draft outreach, and celebrates the new volume. The SDR manager sees more emails sent. The Head of Marketing sees more campaign variations. The CIO sees a cleaner integration between CRM and outreach. The CFO hears that productivity improved because reps are touching more accounts per day.

Then the buyer experience starts to erode.

Messages mention details that are technically public but not actually meaningful. Outreach sounds personalized but feels generic. AI repeats weak proof points, overstates business outcomes, or makes claims the company cannot defend. Customer-success teams start using churn-risk summaries to trigger renewal messages, but account owners do not trust the signals enough to act decisively. Buyers feel processed.

The visible metric improves first.

The trust metric falls later.

This failure pattern is especially dangerous because it looks efficient. A cybersecurity buyer may receive a message that references a recent regulation but ignores the company's actual security posture. A healthcare prospect may get a polished note that sounds relevant but misses the operational problem that really matters. A current customer may receive automated renewal language before support issues are resolved. The system is active, but the decision support is weak.

The boundary redesign is simple.

Do not start with "send more outreach."

Start with "support a better buyer decision."

AI may prepare an account brief, cluster objections, summarize recent calls, compare approved proof points, and draft a follow-up from real account evidence.

AI may not invent urgency, ROI, customer results, competitive claims, security assurances, or compliance promises.

If the company cannot show why this buyer should trust this message, the message should not go out.

A Head of Marketing should ask whether the message is specific, provable, and differentiated.

A CFO should ask whether increased activity produced qualified pipeline, better conversion, or lower customer acquisition waste.

A CIO should ask whether the workflow is drawing from approved CRM and consent-safe data.

A Head of Support or Customer Success leader should ask whether the outreach ignores unresolved service issues that will damage credibility.

A CISO should review any workflow that creates or repeats security, privacy, or compliance-sensitive claims.

Mini-Checklist: Buyer Trust Filter

Before AI-assisted outreach goes live, confirm five things.

Buyer signal:

What real event, objection, pain point, or account change triggered this message?

Approved proof:

What evidence is the message allowed to use?

Claim boundary:

What is AI forbidden to claim, promise, compare, or imply?

Human owner:

Who reviews buyer-facing language before send or publication?

Trust metric:

What metric will show whether trust improved or declined: sales acceptance, reply quality, unsubscribe rate, meeting quality, renewal movement, or customer confidence?

Revenue AI should make buyer decisions easier.

If it makes the company louder but less credible, it is not accelerating revenue.

It is scaling distrust.

Decision Architect's Field Notes

What to Do Next

Choose one revenue workflow where AI is already creating output.

Ask what buyer or customer decision the output is supposed to support.

Then define the approved inputs, human owner, review standard, risk triggers, and success metric.

A good first move is to convert one AI content workflow into an AI evidence workflow. Require proof before draft.

Common Traps to Avoid

Do not measure revenue AI by content volume.

Do not let AI invent proof, claims, outcomes, or customer results.

Do not send AI-personalized messages that are not actually buyer-specific.

Do not confuse faster follow-up with better sales execution.

Do not let customer success summaries replace account judgment.

Boardroom Question

Where is AI increasing revenue activity without improving buyer relevance, proof quality, conversion, retention, or customer trust?

Implementation Law

Revenue AI should not multiply messages. It should improve buyer decisions.

Chapter 16 - The Operational Core

Fulfillment, Production, Support, Service Delivery, and Supply Chain

Operations is where AI promises often meet reality.

The promise is attractive: faster fulfillment, smarter scheduling, better support, fewer delays, cleaner handoffs, improved forecasting, earlier defect detection, and more efficient service delivery.

The risk is also real.

Operations does not run on ideas. It runs on timing, handoffs, capacity, exceptions, people, systems, constraints, and customer promises.

A small AI mistake in operations may not look dramatic at first. It may appear as a delayed order, a missed escalation, an incorrect routing decision, a misunderstood support issue, a poor forecast, a wrong inventory signal, or a small quality defect.

Then the cost spreads.

A customer waits. A technician is assigned incorrectly. A shipment misses a window. A production team works from the wrong assumption. A service issue reopens. A supplier exception is missed. A manager loses confidence in the dashboard.

The blind spot is this:

Operational AI fails when it speeds up tasks without strengthening handoffs, exception handling, and ownership.

Operations is not one workflow. It is a network of dependent workflows. AI must be designed to improve the system, not just one visible step.

The Operational Core Is Built on Handoffs

Most operational failure happens between steps.

The order is entered, but the requirement is unclear.

The ticket is classified, but the escalation rule is weak.

The work is assigned, but the wrong skill is chosen.

The forecast is updated, but nobody trusts it enough to change purchasing.

The defect is detected, but the root cause is not assigned.

The customer is updated, but the promise is too vague.

AI can help with operational handoffs by summarizing, extracting, routing, detecting anomalies, preparing work packets, comparing records, flagging missing information, and recommending next actions.

But the handoff must have a clear owner.

If AI moves work from one step to another without clarity, the workflow may become faster and more fragile.

A good operational AI design asks:

What is being handed off?

Who receives it?

What decision must they make?

What evidence do they need?

What exceptions require escalation?

What happens if the handoff is wrong?

That last question is critical. In operations, the cost of being wrong often appears downstream.

Where AI Helps Operations

AI is strongest in operations when it improves visibility, preparation, and exception detection.

In fulfillment, AI can help identify missing order information, detect unusual requirements, prepare pick-pack instructions, summarize customer constraints, and flag orders likely to miss deadlines.

In production, AI can help analyze defect notes, summarize maintenance logs, detect recurring failure patterns, prepare shift handoff summaries, and flag quality risks.

In support, AI can summarize tickets, extract affected systems, suggest categories, identify missing information, and surface escalation triggers.

In service delivery, AI can prepare work packets, compare customer requirements, analyze technician notes, detect recurring issues, and help managers understand capacity pressure.

In supply chain, AI can monitor supplier updates, summarize disruption signals, compare lead-time changes, flag inventory risk, and prepare exception reports.

But in each case, AI must be tied to a decision.

Should this order move forward?

Should this ticket escalate?

Should this supplier delay trigger action?

Should this defect require root-cause analysis?

Should this job be assigned to this person?

Should this customer receive a revised expectation?

If no decision is defined, AI becomes operational decoration.

Modeled Example: The Support Workflow That Got Faster but Not Cleaner

The following is a modeled example for planning purposes, not an audited client result.

A service organization uses AI to summarize support tickets and suggest routing.

The first month looks good. Summaries appear quickly. Agents spend less time reading long ticket histories. Managers see faster initial handling.

Then the reopen rate rises.

Some tickets were routed correctly by category but incorrectly by context. A billing-related issue included a technical outage. A low-priority request involved a VIP customer. A routine access issue involved a terminated employee. A simple complaint was actually the third repeat incident from the same account.

The AI helped with the visible step: summarization.

It did not solve the operational decision: what should happen next?

The organization redesigns the workflow.

AI now extracts required context before routing: customer tier, repeat issue count, affected system, user role, contract terms, security-sensitive language, prior escalations, and missing information.

The system no longer gives only a category. It gives a routing recommendation with escalation reasons.

If client tier is high, issue repeats, security terms appear, executive users are involved, or missing information blocks safe routing, AI escalates instead of routing automatically.

The team measures resolution time, reopen rate, escalation accuracy, missing-information rate, and customer satisfaction.

The workflow becomes slightly slower at the first step but cleaner across the full process.

That is operational value.

In operations, speed at the front end means little if the back end gets messier.

Implementation Advice for Operations

Start with the handoff that causes the most downstream pain.

Do not start with the task that looks easiest to automate. Start where delays, rework, reopenings, defects, or customer frustration actually appear.

Map the exception path before designing the routine path. Routine cases are usually easy. Exceptions determine whether the workflow scales.

Make missing information visible. AI should not guess when required context is absent. It should flag what is missing.

Separate recommendation from routing. In many operational workflows, AI should recommend first, then act only after the organization proves the boundary is safe.

Measure completed work, not activity. Track reopen rate, rework, delay, defect rate, escalation accuracy, throughput, customer wait time, and cost per completed unit.

Use AI to protect scarce expert attention. AI should prepare the case before experts review it. It should not send experts more noisy summaries.

Design for ordinary users. If the workflow works only when an expert supervises AI, it is not production-ready.

The Operational AI Control Point

Every operational AI workflow needs a control point.

The control point is the moment where the system decides whether the work can continue normally or must escalate.

In fulfillment, the control point may be order completeness.

In support, it may be escalation risk.

In production, it may be quality deviation.

In supply chain, it may be supplier reliability or lead-time change.

In service delivery, it may be whether the assigned resource fits the customer requirement.

The control point should be explicit.

AI should not silently push work forward when required evidence is missing.

A strong control point says:

Proceed because the evidence is complete and risk is low.

Recommend because the evidence is sufficient but human review is needed.

Escalate because risk, uncertainty, or missing context is present.

Stop because the work is outside the approved boundary.

This is how operations gets safer and faster.

Not by letting AI push everything forward.

By letting AI identify what should not move forward yet.

Failure Hotspot: Support Routing and Supply Chain Exceptions

Operational AI usually fails at the edge, not in the middle.

Routine cases often look good in the pilot. The system classifies standard support requests, predicts delivery dates, suggests technician assignment, or summarizes supplier updates. Dashboards improve quickly. The CIO sees smoother workflow automation. The Head of Support sees faster first-touch handling. The CFO sees the possibility of lower cost per case.

Then exceptions begin to leak through.

A support ticket that looks routine is actually the third incident from the same VIP customer. A request categorized as billing is really an outage hidden inside a long thread. A work order is assigned to the wrong technician because the customer requirement was missing from the intake note. A supply chain model predicts normal flow because historical lead times look stable, but a critical supplier changed capacity, shipping terms, or production sequence.

The workflow does not collapse all at once.

It gets noisier downstream.

Reopened tickets increase. Expedites multiply. Managers override the system. Customer frustration rises because the front of the process got faster while the middle of the process got messier.

This is why operational AI should be judged by exception handling, not just routine throughput.

A strong redesign makes the exception gate visible.

In support, AI may summarize every ticket, extract affected systems, count repeat incidents, and recommend routing.

AI should not auto-route when the account is high-value, the issue has repeated, security-sensitive language appears, a multi-user pattern is visible, or required context is missing.

In supply chain, AI may summarize supplier messages, compare lead-time changes, and flag inventory risk.

AI should not quietly normalize disruption when supplier confidence drops, substitute materials appear, delivery terms change, or downstream commitments depend on the order.

A Head of Support should ask whether AI is reducing reopens, not just first-touch time.

A CIO should ask whether the workflow can see the system, contract, and customer context required for safe routing.

A CISO should ask whether identity, access, or security language triggers escalation rather than routine handling.

A CFO should ask whether faster intake really reduces total cost after expedites, rework, and exception review.

A Head of Marketing should ask whether operational promises sent to customers are still credible when exception rates rise.

Mini-Template: The Exception Gate

Exception trigger:

____

What context must be present before AI may route or recommend?

____

What signals force escalation?

____

Who owns the exception queue?

____

What metric proves improvement: reopen rate, expedite rate, delay cost, or customer wait time?

____

Operations becomes safer when AI surfaces what should not move forward yet.

That is the practical test.

If the workflow hides exceptions, speed is only cosmetic.

Decision Architect's Field Notes

What to Do Next

Choose one operational workflow with repeated rework, delays, reopenings, or handoff failures.

Identify the most painful handoff.

Then define the decision made at that handoff, the evidence required, the common exceptions, and the owner.

Design AI to prepare the handoff, not merely accelerate the first step.

Common Traps to Avoid

Do not automate routine flow while ignoring exception flow.

Do not let AI route work without escalation triggers.

Do not measure operational AI by speed alone.

Do not hide missing information.

Do not allow AI to create more downstream cleanup than it removes.

Boardroom Question

Where is AI making operational work move faster while leaving handoffs, exceptions, ownership, and downstream quality unresolved?

Implementation Law

Operational AI scales only when handoffs and exceptions are designed, not guessed.

Chapter 17 - The Financial Shield

Finance, Risk, Compliance, Audit, Insurance, and Portfolio Operations

Finance is where AI claims become harder to exaggerate.

A marketing team may celebrate more content. A support team may celebrate faster summaries. A vendor may celebrate usage. But finance asks a colder question:

What changed in the economics?

Did cost go down?

Did capacity increase?

Did risk decrease?

Did audit readiness improve?

Did cash get protected?

Did margin improve?

Did the company avoid a loss?

Finance, risk, compliance, audit, insurance, and portfolio operations form the Financial Shield of the business. Their job is not to slow the company down for sport. Their job is to prevent avoidable loss, false confidence, weak controls, poor reporting, and unmanaged exposure.

AI can strengthen this shield.

It can also weaken it if implemented casually.

The blind spot is this:

Financial AI becomes dangerous when speed is allowed to outrun control.

In financial systems, a faster mistake is not innovation. It is exposure.

The Financial Shield Is About Control

Finance workflows are full of decisions that look administrative but carry real risk.

Is this invoice valid?

Is this vendor legitimate?

Is this payment routine or unusual?

Is this expense approved?

Is this contract term acceptable?

Is this claim supported?

Is this portfolio company's AI initiative producing value or just activity?

Is this exception material?

Is this audit trail complete?

AI can assist with extraction, reconciliation, anomaly detection, policy comparison, document summarization, fraud signal review, and reporting preparation.

But finance should be careful about allowing AI to act directly on high-risk decisions.

The Financial Shield requires three disciplines:

Evidence before approval.

Escalation before exposure.

Auditability before scale.

If AI cannot show why something was classified, routed, flagged, or recommended, the workflow is not ready for high-trust financial use.

Where AI Helps the Financial Shield

In finance operations, AI can extract invoice fields, compare purchase orders, summarize vendor histories, identify missing approvals, flag changed payment details, and prepare exception packets.

In risk and compliance, AI can summarize policy changes, identify control gaps, compare documentation, organize evidence, and highlight unusual patterns.

In audit, AI can prepare documentation, trace decisions, identify missing records, and help reviewers focus on exceptions.

In insurance, AI can summarize claims, extract risk factors, compare policy language, and organize underwriting or renewal information for review.

In portfolio operations, AI can compare operating metrics across companies, identify inconsistent reporting, analyze AI initiative claims, and help operators distinguish real productivity from activity.

But in all cases, AI should support human control.

It should not hide uncertainty behind clean language.

It should not convert incomplete evidence into approval.

It should not average away exceptions.

It should not treat low-risk and high-risk decisions as the same.

Modeled Example: The Invoice Workflow That Needed a Shield

The following is a modeled example for planning purposes, not an audited client result.

A finance team uses AI to accelerate invoice processing.

At first, the results look strong. AI extracts vendor name, invoice number, amount, date, payment terms, and purchase order reference. Routine invoices move faster. Analysts like the reduced data entry.

Then a near-miss appears.

An invoice from an existing vendor is marked routine. The vendor name matches. The amount is ordinary. The format is familiar.

But the payment instructions changed.

The analyst sees the routine label and moves quickly. The manager approves the batch. Later, finance discovers that changed payment details should have triggered separate verification.

The AI did not approve the payment.

But it influenced the review path.

That distinction matters.

The workflow is redesigned around the Financial Shield.

AI may extract fields and compare records.

AI may recommend routine or exception status.

AI may prepare a review packet.

AI may not approve payment.

AI may not classify an invoice as routine when bank details, vendor tax information, address, ownership, approval path, or payment timing changes.

Changed payment instructions automatically create a high-risk exception.

The audit trail records the exception trigger, reviewer, verification step, approver, and decision time.

Now AI supports control instead of weakening it.

The workflow still gets faster for routine invoices.

But risky cases receive the attention they deserve.

That is financial implementation discipline.

The CFO and Compliance View

The CFO is not asking AI teams to stop experimenting.

The CFO is asking them to stop making unsupported claims.

A CFO-friendly AI business case explains:

Which workflow changes.

Which cost or risk is affected.

Which control remains human-owned.

Which evidence is preserved.

Which new costs appear.

Which metric proves improvement.

Which failure mode would stop the project.

Compliance leaders ask related questions:

Can we explain the decision later?

Can we show who reviewed it?

Can we prove the policy was followed?

Can we identify exceptions?

Can we demonstrate that AI did not approve what humans were supposed to own?

If the answer is no, the workflow may be useful but not yet controlled.

In high-trust business systems, usefulness is not enough.

The organization must be able to defend the decision.

AI in Portfolio Operations

Private equity, venture operators, and multi-location business owners should treat AI as a portfolio discipline, not a collection of isolated experiments.

A portfolio operator should not only ask, "Which company is using AI?"

The better questions are:

Which workflows are being improved?

What evidence supports the claimed improvement?

What costs are hidden?

What risks are created?

Which initiatives are repeatable across the portfolio?

Which should stop?

AI can help portfolio operators compare operating patterns across companies. But the portfolio office must avoid accepting AI productivity stories without financial translation.

One portfolio company may claim AI saves time in customer support. Another may claim AI improves marketing. Another may claim AI speeds reporting.

The portfolio operator should ask each one for the same evidence standard:

Workflow.

Decision.

Baseline.

AI role.

Human owner.

Risk level.

Rework cost.

Operating metric.

Financial path.

Scale-or-stop recommendation.

This creates comparability.

Without a shared evidence standard, AI reporting becomes theater at portfolio scale.

Implementation Advice for the Financial Shield

Never start financial AI with approval automation.

Start with evidence preparation, exception detection, and review support.

Define exception triggers before testing. Examples include changed bank details, new vendors, unusual amounts, missing purchase orders, duplicate invoice signals, rushed payment requests, contract deviations, unsupported claims, or missing approvals.

Separate routine processing from high-risk decisions. AI may help routine work move faster, but exceptions should become more visible, not less.

Preserve audit trails. Important AI-influenced decisions should record output, evidence, reviewer, final decision, and exception reason.

Do not let AI produce financial claims without operational proof. If an AI project claims savings, require the pathway: cost reduction, capacity, margin protection, revenue, or risk-adjusted value.

Give compliance a role early. Compliance should not appear only after the pilot is celebrated.

Use AI to reduce blind spots, not create new ones.

Failure Hotspot: Finance AI That Overclaims Savings

Finance AI rarely fails because extraction is impossible.

It fails because economics are overstated before exception costs are measured.

A team pilots AI for invoice extraction, expense review, policy matching, claims summarization, or portfolio reporting. The visible gain looks obvious. Forms are read faster. Packets are prepared faster. Analysts spend less time typing. The CIO sees a cleaner workflow. The

CFO hears that processing time fell sharply. A business unit leader starts repeating the savings number in meetings.

That is usually where the trouble starts.

The pilot saved time on the easy cases. It did not remove the expensive work.

Changed bank details still require verification. Unusual vendors still require review. Missing approvals still create delay. Policy exceptions still need judgment. Audit trails still need to be preserved. Portfolio companies still report "AI savings" in different ways, making comparisons weak or impossible.

If leadership books the gross time reduction as ROI, the finance function becomes the place where AI credibility breaks.

The redesign is not complicated.

Separate the workflow into lanes.

Routine lane:

AI may extract, compare, reconcile, and prepare a normal review packet.

Exception lane:

AI may flag inconsistencies, missing approvals, changed payment details, policy deviations, duplicate signals, or unusual patterns.

High-risk lane:

AI must escalate items involving money movement changes, new vendors, unusual amounts, compliance-sensitive exceptions, or unsupported financial claims.

AI should not approve high-risk decisions. It should accelerate evidence and make exceptions visible.

A CFO should ask whether the claimed savings survive review time, exception handling, duplicate detection, and audit preparation.

A CIO should ask whether the financial workflow preserves source evidence, reviewer identity, and system traceability.

A CISO should ask whether payment-detail changes, identity anomalies, or data-access risks are properly separated from routine processing.

A Head of Support or operations leader should ask whether any capacity claim reflects completed work, not just faster intake.

A Head of Marketing should not publish ROI language from a finance AI initiative until finance signs off on the operating path.

Mini-Checklist: CFO Proof Standard

Claimed gain:

What changed in cost, capacity, margin, cash protection, or risk?

Lane split:

What share of volume is routine, exception, and high-risk?

Net value:

What remains after verification, correction, exception handling, and monitoring?

Control:

What did AI influence, and what did humans still approve?

Evidence:

Can audit, compliance, or the board reconstruct the decision later?

Finance AI becomes valuable when it is harder to exaggerate than to defend.

That is how the Financial Shield keeps AI honest.

Decision Architect's Field Notes

What to Do Next

Choose one financial, risk, compliance, audit, insurance, or portfolio workflow.

Identify where AI could prepare evidence, detect exceptions, reduce review burden, or improve audit readiness.

Then define what AI must not approve.

Write the exception triggers before running the pilot.

Common Traps to Avoid

Do not let AI approve high-risk financial decisions.

Do not treat extraction accuracy as approval readiness.

Do not ignore changed payment details, unusual vendors, or missing approvals.

Do not make financial ROI claims without showing the operating path.

Do not scale without audit trail design.

Boardroom Question

Where can AI strengthen financial control, risk visibility, and audit readiness without taking ownership of decisions humans must still own?

Implementation Law

Financial AI should accelerate evidence, not bypass control.

Chapter 18 - High-Risk Environments

Cybersecurity, Healthcare, and Regulated AI

High-risk environments expose the weakness of vague AI strategy.

In low-risk work, a flawed AI draft may waste time. In high-risk work, a flawed AI-influenced decision can affect security, patient trust, privacy, compliance, safety, money, legal exposure, or business continuity.

This does not mean AI should be avoided.

It means AI must be designed with stronger discipline.

Cybersecurity teams can use AI to summarize alerts, enrich investigations, cluster incidents, draft reports, and reduce analyst reading burden.

Healthcare administrators can use AI to summarize records, draft non-clinical communications, organize scheduling issues, identify missing documentation, and reduce administrative friction.

Regulated organizations can use AI to compare policies, prepare evidence, detect exceptions, and support review workflows.

But high-risk AI must be built around boundaries.

The blind spot is this:

Organizations often use low-risk AI habits inside high-risk systems.

That is where trouble begins.

A prompt that is acceptable for brainstorming is not acceptable for a security response. A draft that is acceptable for internal notes is not acceptable for regulated customer communication. A summary that is useful for orientation is not enough for clinical, legal, financial, or compliance-sensitive decisions.

High-risk environments require a different standard.

The High-Risk Rule

The high-risk rule is simple:

AI may prepare evidence faster than humans, but humans must own high-consequence decisions.

That does not make AI weak.

It makes AI useful in the right lane.

In cybersecurity, AI may summarize an alert, gather related signals, identify possible severity, and prepare an incident brief. But human analysts should own escalation and response decisions for high-risk incidents.

In healthcare administration, AI may draft a scheduling message, summarize administrative records, or identify missing paperwork. But it should not make clinical judgments or override privacy and role boundaries.

In regulated AI workflows, AI may compare documents, flag missing evidence, and organize review packets. But humans must own legal interpretation, compliance approval, customer commitments, and material decisions.

The stronger the consequence, the stronger the human ownership.

Cybersecurity: AI as Analyst Leverage, Not Autopilot Cybersecurity teams are overloaded with alerts, logs, reports, tickets, threat notes, vendor messages, and incident documentation.

AI can help.

It can reduce reading burden. It can summarize long event histories. It can correlate repeated signals. It can draft incident notes. It can prepare evidence for review. It can help junior analysts understand context faster.

But cybersecurity is full of asymmetric risk.

A false positive wastes time.

A false negative can become a serious incident.

An automated containment action can disrupt the business if triggered incorrectly.

Therefore, the best early cybersecurity AI use cases are usually evidence preparation and analyst leverage, not autonomous response.

A practical cybersecurity boundary may look like this:

AI may assist by summarizing alerts and gathering evidence.

AI may recommend severity with visible reasons.

AI may not downgrade high-risk alerts without review.

AI may not independently ignore repeated signals.

AI may not trigger disruptive containment actions outside approved playbooks.

AI must escalate when privileged users, sensitive systems, lateral movement, unusual geography, repeated alerts, or unclear asset criticality appear.

This gives AI a strong role without giving it unsafe authority.

Healthcare Administration: Reduce Burden Without Crossing the Line

Healthcare administration is full of paperwork, scheduling, documentation, patient communication, insurance coordination, and compliance-sensitive handling of information.

AI can help reduce administrative burden.

But healthcare is also full of trust, privacy, role boundaries, and regulatory exposure.

A useful healthcare administration AI workflow may help summarize non-clinical records, identify missing intake information, prepare appointment instructions, organize insurance documentation, or draft administrative messages for review.

The boundary must be explicit.

AI may assist with administrative summarization.

AI may draft non-clinical communication.

AI may identify missing documentation.

AI may recommend routing to the correct administrative team.

AI should not provide clinical judgment unless it is inside a properly approved clinical system with professional oversight.

AI should not expose sensitive information outside approved channels.

AI should not send patient-facing messages without role-appropriate review when the content affects care, billing, privacy, or rights.

The point is not fear.

The point is role clarity.

In healthcare, a helpful administrative assistant becomes dangerous when it starts acting like an unauthorized decision-maker.

Regulated AI: Evidence Before Automation

Regulated environments include finance, insurance, healthcare, cybersecurity, legal, government contracting, education, employment, and other areas where decisions may be reviewed by auditors, regulators, customers, boards, or courts.

In these environments, AI implementation must preserve evidence.

The question is not only:

Did AI help?

The question is:

Can we explain what happened later?

A regulated AI workflow should record the input, output, reviewer, final decision, source evidence, exception reason, and escalation path when the decision is material.

This does not mean every small internal AI use requires heavy documentation. Risk level matters.

But when AI influences decisions involving money, access, eligibility, claims, compliance, security, healthcare administration, employment, or customer commitments, the organization must be able to reconstruct the decision.

If it cannot, the Shadow Ledger grows.

Modeled Example: The Cybersecurity Alert That Looked Routine

The following is a modeled example for planning purposes, not an audited client result.

A cybersecurity team uses AI to summarize endpoint alerts.

The pilot performs well. Analysts like the concise summaries. The tool reduces reading time and helps junior analysts understand event histories.

One alert is summarized as likely low priority because it resembles previous benign activity.

But the summary does not clearly highlight that the user has elevated privileges and the device connects to sensitive systems.

The analyst reviews quickly and leaves the alert in the queue.

Later, related activity appears.

The problem is not that AI summarized the alert.

The problem is that the workflow did not require escalation when privileged identity and sensitive asset context appeared.

The team redesigns the boundary.

AI may summarize all alerts.

AI may recommend severity only when asset criticality, user privilege, related alerts, and known business context are included.

AI must escalate when privileged users, sensitive systems, repeated signals, lateral movement, unusual geography, or missing asset data appears.

The alert summary must show escalation reasons at the top.

The analyst remains the owner of severity and response.

The result is not full automation.

It is better analyst leverage with stronger risk control.

That is the correct direction for high-risk AI.

Implementation Advice for High-Risk Environments

Start with evidence preparation, not autonomous action.

Use AI to reduce reading burden, organize facts, detect missing information, and prepare review packets.

Define stop rules before deployment.

Stop when data is missing, risk is high, context is unclear, or the requested action crosses role boundaries.

Make escalation visible.

Do not bury risk signals in long summaries. High-risk triggers should appear at the top of the workflow.

Preserve audit trails for material decisions.

Record what AI produced, what evidence was used, who reviewed it, what decision was made, and why escalation did or did not occur.

Separate administrative assistance from professional judgment.

This matters especially in healthcare, law, finance, compliance, and cybersecurity.

Train users on boundaries, not just tools.

Employees should know not only how to use AI, but what AI is not allowed to do.

Failure Hotspot: Agentic AI Without Stop Rules

The most dangerous agentic AI mistake is not autonomy by itself.

It is autonomy without a hard boundary.

An organization gives an agent access to inboxes, ticketing systems, knowledge bases, CRM records, or security tools. The promise sounds attractive: let the agent gather information, decide the next step, update the record, send the message, and close the loop.

In low-risk environments, that may be manageable.

In high-risk environments, a missing stop rule can turn a useful assistant into an unowned decision-maker.

A CISO may approve a security agent to enrich alerts, but the team never writes the point at which the agent must stop and escalate. A CIO may allow an operations agent to move across systems, but nobody defines which tools are read-only and which actions are reversible. A CFO may support the pilot because it appears to reduce labor, but the economic model never includes incident cleanup, customer impact, or compliance exposure. A Head of Support may like the faster case handling until the agent closes a sensitive case without surfacing the real exception. A Head of Marketing or communications lead may discover that the agent drafted external language before the facts were stable.

That is why stop rules deserve their own design step.

A stop rule is not a vague statement that "humans remain responsible."

A stop rule is a written condition that prevents the agent from proceeding.

For example:

Stop if the case involves privileged identity, payment movement, regulated data, legal interpretation, patient rights, or customer commitments.

Stop if the required evidence is incomplete.

Stop if the model cannot explain the reason for the recommendation in business language.

Stop if the action would be difficult to reverse.

Stop if the workflow crosses from internal preparation into external commitment.

Mini-Template: Agentic Stop-Rule Sheet

Agent name or workflow:

____

Allowed actions:

____

Read-only systems:

____

Actions requiring human approval:

____

Triggers that force stop or escalation:

____

Owner on call:

____

Log and audit record required:

____

A useful agent is not the one that can do the most.

In a high-risk environment, the useful agent is the one that knows exactly where its authority ends.

That is what makes the workflow safer, more defensible, and more likely to scale.

Decision Architect's Field Notes

What to Do Next

Choose one high-risk AI use case.

Before testing, define the consequence of being wrong.

Then define AI's allowed role, the human owner, the required evidence, the escalation triggers, and the stop conditions.

If those cannot be written clearly, the use case is not ready.

Common Traps to Avoid

Do not use low-risk AI habits in high-risk workflows.

Do not let AI downgrade security, compliance, financial, healthcare, or legal risk without human ownership.

Do not hide escalation signals inside long summaries.

Do not deploy without audit trail requirements.

Do not confuse administrative support with professional judgment.

Boardroom Question

Where is AI already influencing high-risk decisions without the ownership, evidence, escalation, and auditability those decisions require?

Implementation Law

In high-risk environments, AI should prepare evidence faster, not own consequences humans must control.

Part V - Compact Hard-Dollar Case Studies

These case studies are designed to make the book's ideas concrete. They are not meant to prove universal ROI. They show how AI economics change when the organization counts review burden, exception handling, ownership, decision boundaries, and total cost.

Each case follows the same structure: setup, baseline, AI intervention, Rework Tax, what went wrong, decision boundary redesign, revised economics, and lesson.

Why These Nine Cases Matter Now

These nine cases were not chosen because they are dramatic.

They were chosen because they repeat.

Across industries, functions, and tools, weak AI implementations usually fail in recognizable patterns. The vendor changes. The dashboard changes. The promise changes. The failure pattern usually does not.

The first pattern is **false speed**.

Work gets faster at the visible step, but the completed workflow is not actually cheaper, cleaner, safer, or more reliable. The MSP case shows this clearly. Ticket triage improved at the front of the workflow, but senior review, exception handling, client-specific context, and reopen risk absorbed much of the gain. The Head of Support sees this as noisy operations. The CIO sees it as a workflow-quality problem. The CFO sees it as a margin story that was claimed too early.

The second pattern is **pilot success without production readiness**.

The cybersecurity case matters because it shows the difference between evidence preparation and autonomous response. The pilot helped analysts read faster. It did not prove that the team could safely automate response actions. This is the gap many CIOs, CISOs, and security leaders face now: a useful assistive tool, a strong demo, and no safe case yet for expanding authority.

The third pattern is **output inflation that damages trust**.

The marketing case matters because AI often makes communication teams louder before it makes them more credible. A Head of Marketing may see more drafts, more campaigns, and more activity. But buyers do not pay for volume. They respond to relevance, proof, differentiation, and trust. The CFO eventually asks the harder question: what changed in conversion, pipeline quality, retention, margin, or wasted spend?

The fourth pattern is **ROI overclaim**.

The finance case matters because finance is where loose AI math finally gets challenged. Time saved on routine cases is not the same as net value across routine work, exceptions, controls, approvals, and audit readiness. This is why CFOs become central to good AI implementation, not because they resist AI, but because they force the economics to become real.

The fifth pattern is **strategic stopping**.

Some AI projects should stop. Not because AI is bad, but because the workflow is not ready, the data is weak, the ownership is unclear, the risk is too high, or the value does not justify production effort. Knowing when to stop is not a lack of innovation. It is one of the clearest marks of operating discipline.

The sixth pattern is **environmental mismatch**.

The manufacturing case matters because AI can look useful in a clean planning meeting and fail under real operating conditions. Plant floors, service environments, logistics systems, warehouses, and field operations do not behave like polished demos. Noise, timing, handoffs, safety rules, machine constraints, shift changes, and exception-heavy work can destroy a weak AI design. The lesson is simple: AI must survive the environment where the work actually happens.

The seventh pattern is **customer-facing friction hidden behind internal efficiency**.

The chatbot case matters because reducing tickets is not the same as improving service. A chatbot can make the company's dashboard look better while making the customer's experience worse. If customers are forced through weak automation, repeat themselves, escalate angrily, or lose trust, the apparent savings may become retention risk. Customer service AI must be measured by resolution quality, customer effort, escalation accuracy, and trust — not only by deflection.

The eighth pattern is **boundary confusion in high-risk workflows**.

The healthcare case matters because some workflows look administrative until they touch patient safety, privacy, clinical meaning, insurance access, consent, or regulated communication. AI may prepare evidence, summarize records, and reduce routine burden, but it must know when to stop. In high-risk environments, the most important AI feature may not be generation. It may be escalation.

The ninth pattern is **portfolio-level AI theater**.

The venture capital case matters because investors, boards, and portfolio operators need a better way to separate AI activity from enterprise value. A company can use AI everywhere and still fail to improve margin, growth, retention, defensibility, or operating leverage. Portfolio leaders do not need more AI stories. They need investor-grade evidence: which workflow improved, what metric changed, what rework remained, what risk was created, and whether the initiative deserves scale.

Read these cases as operating mirrors.

If you lead support, begin with the MSP and chatbot cases.

If you own cybersecurity or regulated workflows, begin with the cybersecurity and healthcare cases.

If you lead demand generation, brand, sales, or customer communications, begin with the marketing case.

If you carry financial accountability, begin with the finance case.

If you run operations, production, fulfillment, or field service, begin with the manufacturing case.

If you manage a portfolio of AI experiments, business units, or portfolio companies, begin with the stopping and venture portfolio cases.

Mini-Checklist: Which Failure Pattern Looks Most Like Us?

Are we faster at the first step but not cheaper or cleaner at the completed workflow?

Did the pilot look good without proving safe production use?

Has AI increased output while weakening trust, differentiation, or customer confidence?

Have we claimed savings before counting review, correction, exceptions, controls, and audit burden?

Are we keeping an AI project alive because nobody wants to admit it should stop?

Did the AI design work in a clean test but fail in the real operating environment?

Are we reducing internal workload while increasing customer frustration?

Are we treating a high-risk workflow as simple because the first task looks administrative?

Are we reporting AI activity without proving impact on margin, growth, retention, risk, or enterprise value?

These nine cases matter now because they turn abstract AI optimism into recognizable operational choices.

That is what most teams need next.

Not another theory of AI.

A clearer way to see the failure pattern they are already living inside.

Case 1 - The MSP That Got Faster but Not Cheaper

Setup

A regional managed service provider wanted to improve service desk efficiency. Ticket volume had increased, technicians were overloaded, and leadership wanted faster triage without hiring immediately.

The company approved an AI feature inside its ticketing platform. The goal was simple: summarize incoming tickets, suggest categories, and recommend routing.

The pilot looked promising. AI summaries appeared quickly. Level 1 technicians spent less time reading long ticket threads. Managers saw faster first-touch activity.

The first internal report said the workflow was working.

Baseline

Before AI, a Level 1 technician spent about six minutes reading, summarizing, classifying, and routing an average ticket.

The MSP handled about 3,000 tickets per month.

At first glance, the cost problem looked clear. If AI could reduce triage time by even three minutes per ticket, the MSP could free 150 hours per month.

That sounded like a meaningful operational gain.

AI Intervention

The AI system summarized the ticket history, suggested a category, proposed priority, and recommended routing.

For routine tickets, it helped. Password resets, basic access issues, software questions, and simple printer problems moved faster.

The problem appeared in mixed-context tickets.

Some tickets looked routine but were not. A "slow computer" ticket included endpoint protection warnings. A "login issue" involved a recently terminated employee. A "printer problem" was actually a network issue affecting several users. A "simple access request" involved an executive account.

The AI did not understand the MSP's business context deeply enough.

Rework Tax

The MSP's initial claim was that AI saved three to four minutes per ticket.

But senior technicians began checking many summaries because misclassification could create client risk.

The Rework Tax included:

technician verification of summaries

correction of wrong categories

escalation review for security-sensitive tickets

reopened tickets caused by weak routing

manager time spent resolving classification disputes

The MSP had gained speed at Level 1 but increased review pressure at Level 2 and Level 3.

The workflow was faster at the front end but not cheaper across the whole service system.

What Went Wrong

The use case was too broad.

The MSP treated ticket triage as one task. In reality, triage contained several decisions:

What is the issue?

Who is affected?

Is the client high priority?

Is there security exposure?

Is this an outage?

Does the contract change the response requirement?

Can AI route this safely, or should it escalate?

The AI was asked to classify before the decision boundary was designed.

Decision Boundary Redesign

The redesigned workflow separated tickets into three lanes.

Low-risk lane: AI may summarize and route narrow ticket types such as password resets, routine access questions, and basic software support.

Review lane: AI may summarize and recommend routing, but a technician reviews before assignment.

Escalation lane: AI must escalate when tickets mention suspicious login behavior, endpoint protection alerts, executive users, backup failure, multi-user outages, terminated employees, identity changes, or missing client context.

AI was no longer judged by whether it could "triage tickets."

It was judged by whether it could reduce low-value work while protecting escalation quality.

Revised Economics

The MSP stopped claiming full labor savings.

The revised value case became more accurate:

Level 1 triage time decreased for low-risk tickets.

Senior review burden declined after escalation rules improved.

Reopen rate dropped because context-sensitive tickets were routed more carefully.

The MSP avoided immediate hiring as routine volume grew.

Service margin improved only where review burden fell and ticket quality held steady.

The financial story changed from "AI saves 150 hours per month" to:

"AI improves service margin when it reduces low-risk triage time without increasing senior review, reopen rates, or client risk."

That is a much stronger business case.

Lesson

The MSP did not need full automation. It needed controlled routing.

AI became useful when it stopped pretending every ticket was the same.

Implementation lesson: In MSPs, AI should summarize broadly, recommend carefully, route narrowly, and escalate aggressively.

Case 2 - The Cybersecurity Pilot That Could Not Automate Response

Setup

A cybersecurity team wanted to reduce analyst overload. Alerts were increasing, analysts were tired, and leadership wanted AI to help triage incidents faster.

The team tested AI to summarize endpoint alerts, group related signals, suggest severity, and recommend response actions.

The demo looked strong. Analysts liked the concise summaries. Junior team members said the AI made complex alert histories easier to understand.

Leadership asked whether the system could eventually automate parts of response.

That question exposed the real problem.

Baseline

Before AI, analysts spent significant time reading alert details, checking endpoint history, reviewing user activity, and deciding whether to escalate.

The baseline pain was not only alert volume.

The real pain was evidence gathering.

Analysts were not slow because they were careless. They were slow because each meaningful decision required context: asset criticality, user privilege, prior activity, business impact, related alerts, and containment risk.

AI Intervention

AI summarized alerts and suggested likely severity.

For simple low-risk alerts, this helped. Analysts could orient faster.

But cybersecurity is not a normal productivity workflow. A wrong decision can create serious consequences.

One alert was summarized as likely low priority because it resembled prior benign activity. The summary did not clearly highlight that the user had elevated privileges and the device connected to sensitive systems.

The analyst did not ignore the alert because of AI alone. But the AI summary influenced the review path.

The alert stayed in the queue longer than it should have.

Rework Tax

The Rework Tax was not only correction time.

It included:

analyst verification of AI summaries

checking whether critical context was missing

re-review of downgraded alerts

manager review for response recommendations

documentation cleanup

time spent debating whether AI severity labels could be trusted

The AI reduced reading time but did not reduce response ownership.

The team could not safely automate response based on the pilot.

What Went Wrong

The team confused alert summarization with response readiness.

Summarization was useful.

Automated response was a different risk category.

The AI could organize evidence, but it could not own severity judgment or containment decisions without strict boundaries.

The pilot was designed around output quality, not decision ownership.

Decision Boundary Redesign

The redesigned cybersecurity workflow separated AI roles:

Assist: AI may summarize alerts, collect related signals, identify missing evidence, and prepare incident briefs.

Recommend: AI may suggest severity only when it shows visible reasons: asset criticality, user privilege, related alerts, known behavior, and business impact.

Escalate: AI must escalate when privileged accounts, sensitive systems, repeated signals, lateral movement indicators, unusual geography, or missing asset data appear.

Stop: AI may not independently downgrade high-risk alerts, ignore repeated signals, or trigger disruptive containment outside approved playbooks.

The analyst remained the owner of severity and response.

Revised Economics

The revised business case no longer claimed response automation.

It claimed analyst leverage.

That was more realistic and more valuable.

The team measured:

time to understand alert context

missing-evidence rate

escalation accuracy

analyst review burden

incident documentation quality

false-positive handling time

response readiness

The project still had value, but the value was not "AI replaces analysts."

The value was:

"AI prepares evidence faster so analysts can make better decisions with less reading burden."

Lesson

Cybersecurity AI should not begin as autopilot.

It should begin as analyst leverage.

Implementation lesson: In cybersecurity, AI can accelerate evidence preparation, but response ownership must stay human unless the action is narrow, approved, reversible, and governed by a tested playbook.

Case 3 - The Marketing Team That Doubled Output and Lost Trust

Setup

A B2B marketing team adopted AI to increase campaign output. The team was small, the content calendar was overloaded, and leadership wanted more visibility in the market.

AI seemed like an obvious solution.

Within weeks, the team was producing more blog drafts, LinkedIn posts, landing page copy, email campaigns, webinar descriptions, and sales-support material.

The dashboard looked better.

The market response did not.

Baseline

Before AI, the team produced about eight major campaign assets per month.

The bottleneck appeared to be production capacity. Marketing could not create enough content to support every product, segment, campaign, and sales request.

Leadership assumed more output would create more opportunity.

That assumption was only partly true.

The real bottleneck was not content production.

The real bottleneck was buyer relevance.

AI Intervention

AI helped the team create drafts quickly.

Output doubled. In some weeks, it tripled.

But the drafts began sounding similar. Claims were polished but generic. Some messages could have applied to almost any competitor. Sales complained that the content did not reflect real buyer conversations. Legal flagged unsupported claims. The CEO said the company was publishing more but sounding less distinct.

The AI did what it was asked to do.

The team had asked it to produce content.

It should have asked AI to support better GTM decisions.

Rework Tax

The Rework Tax appeared in several places:

brand review increased

sales rejected more assets

legal flagged more claims

marketers rewrote generic copy

managers spent more time deciding which drafts were usable

customer-facing messaging became less differentiated

The team had more content but weaker trust.

That is a dangerous trade.

What Went Wrong

The team measured volume instead of buyer movement.

It counted drafts, posts, emails, and campaigns.

It did not measure whether the content improved buyer understanding, sales acceptance, qualified response, or trust.

AI became a content inflation machine.

The implementation lacked a decision boundary around claims, proof, and buyer relevance.

Decision Boundary Redesign

The team redesigned AI's role.

AI would no longer begin with "write a campaign."

It would begin with a campaign evidence pack.

The evidence pack included:

target buyer segment

buyer pain

approved positioning

proof points

customer objections

sales-call notes

product limitations

competitor pressure

compliance constraints

approved claims

AI's role shifted from content generator to campaign brief assistant.

AI could draft a structured campaign brief.

AI could suggest message angles.

AI could identify missing proof.

AI could flag unsupported claims.

AI could not invent customer results, pricing promises, compliance claims, competitive comparisons, or ROI numbers.

Human owners remained responsible for proof, positioning, brand voice, and publication.

Revised Economics

The revised economics were not based on content volume.

They were based on better revenue work:

fewer major rewrites

higher sales acceptance

fewer legal claim defects

better campaign readiness

improved buyer-specific relevance

stronger qualified response

less wasted content production

The team produced fewer assets than during the content explosion, but the assets were more usable.

The business case changed from:

"AI tripled marketing output."

To:

"AI reduces campaign preparation time and improves message quality when it works from approved buyer evidence."

That is a better claim.

Lesson

Marketing AI should not be measured by how much it writes.

It should be measured by whether it improves buyer decisions.

Implementation lesson: If AI increases content volume while weakening proof, differentiation, or trust, the workflow is not scaling marketing. It is scaling noise.

Case 4 - The Finance Workflow That Almost Overclaimed ROI

Setup

A finance team wanted to use AI to process invoices faster.

The pilot focused on field extraction, purchase order matching, vendor comparison, and routine classification.

The first results looked promising. AI reduced manual typing. Routine invoices moved faster. Analysts liked the cleaner review packets.

Leadership saw a possible hard-dollar ROI story.

The CFO was interested but cautious.

Baseline

Before AI, a routine invoice review took about ten minutes.

The finance team processed a high volume of invoices each month.

The initial assumption was simple: if AI reduced routine invoice time from ten minutes to four minutes, the company could claim six minutes saved per invoice.

That looked like a strong productivity case.

But the baseline mixed routine invoices and exceptions.

That was the problem.

AI Intervention

AI extracted invoice fields, compared purchase orders, matched vendors, and suggested whether an invoice looked routine.

For clean invoices, the system helped.

But exceptions still required human attention: changed bank details, missing purchase orders, new vendors, duplicate invoice signals, unusual amounts, mismatched approval paths, and rushed payment requests.

The AI improved the easiest part of the workflow.

It did not eliminate the expensive part.

Rework Tax

The Rework Tax included:

analyst verification of extracted fields

review of exception flags

investigation of vendor changes

manager approval for unusual payments

audit trail cleanup

correction of false routine classifications

compliance review for high-risk items

The original ROI model counted generation speed but undercounted exception handling.

This created a risk of overclaiming ROI.

What Went Wrong

The finance team almost made a common mistake: averaging routine processing gains across the whole workflow.

Routine invoices improved.

Exception-heavy invoices did not improve enough.

Some became more sensitive because AI labels could lower reviewer attention.

The problem was not that AI failed.

The problem was that the ROI claim was too broad.

The AI should not have been sold as "invoice automation."

It should have been positioned as routine extraction plus exception visibility.

Decision Boundary Redesign

The redesigned workflow separated three lanes.

Routine lane: AI extracts fields, compares known records, and prepares standard review when vendor, amount, purchase order, approval path, and payment details match.

Exception lane: AI flags missing or mismatched information and prepares a review packet for analysts.

High-risk lane: AI must escalate changed bank details, new vendors, unusual amounts, duplicate signals, rushed payment requests, or approval path changes.

AI may not approve payments.

AI may not label an invoice as routine if payment instructions changed.

AI must show the reason for routine or exception status.

The approval record must preserve exception trigger, reviewer, final approver, and decision time.

Revised Economics

The revised ROI became more honest.

The team separated routine invoices from exceptions.

It measured:

extraction time

review time

exception rate

payment delay

audit cleanup

duplicate-risk detection

senior review burden

cost per completed invoice by category

The financial story changed from:

"AI saves six minutes per invoice."

To:

"AI reduces routine processing time and improves exception visibility, but ROI depends on exception rate, review burden, and payment-risk controls."

That is less dramatic but much more defensible.

The CFO could work with that.

Lesson

Finance AI should not overclaim automation before exception economics are measured.

Implementation lesson: In finance, AI may accelerate evidence and routine processing, but ROI must be calculated separately for routine work, exceptions, and high-risk approvals.

Case 5 - The AI Project That Needed to Stop

Setup

A mid-market company launched an AI initiative to automate executive reporting.

Every week, managers spent hours collecting updates, summarizing department activity, preparing slides, and answering leadership questions.

The AI project promised to generate executive reports automatically from project management tools, CRM notes, support tickets, finance summaries, and meeting transcripts.

The idea sounded valuable.

The pilot looked impressive.

The project still needed to stop.

Baseline

Before AI, the weekly report took about twelve hours across several managers.

The process was frustrating. Data came from too many systems. Updates were inconsistent. Some managers wrote too much. Others wrote too little. The CEO complained that the report showed activity but not real business risk.

The team assumed AI could fix the reporting burden.

But the real problem was not writing.

The real problem was unclear management discipline.

AI Intervention

AI pulled information from multiple sources and produced a clean weekly summary.

The output looked professional. It grouped updates by department, highlighted open issues, and drafted executive bullets.

Leadership liked the format.

Then they read more carefully.

Some updates were technically accurate but strategically misleading. The AI summarized activity without understanding priority. It treated minor tasks and material risks with similar weight. It repeated optimistic manager language without challenge. It missed weak signals buried in support tickets. It created a polished report that still did not answer the CEO's real question:

"What should I pay attention to?"

Rework Tax

The Rework Tax was heavy.

Managers had to verify the summaries.

Department heads corrected context.

Finance checked numbers.

Operations clarified risk.

The CEO still asked follow-up questions because the report did not separate activity from decision relevance.

The AI saved drafting time but increased trust review.

The workflow did not improve enough.

What Went Wrong

The company tried to automate reporting before defining executive decision needs.

The weekly report was not just a document.

It supported decisions about risk, resources, accountability, escalation, customer issues, hiring, cash, and priorities.

AI had no clear standard for what mattered.

It summarized what was available instead of surfacing what leadership needed.

The pilot created a better-looking report, not a better management system.

Decision Boundary Redesign

The team attempted a redesign.

AI would not generate the final report.

It would prepare evidence packets by department.

Each packet would include:

key metric changes

open risks

overdue decisions

customer-impacting issues

resource constraints

unresolved escalations

confidence level of source data

missing updates

Department owners would be responsible for final interpretation.

AI would flag missing or stale data.

AI would not assign priority without human review.

This redesign was better.

But another problem appeared.

The underlying source systems were too inconsistent. Managers used different definitions for status. Key metrics were not updated reliably. Some critical information lived in private notes and informal conversations.

AI could not fix a reporting system that leadership had not standardized.

Revised Economics

The revised economics did not justify scale.

The project could save some drafting time, but only after major process cleanup, data standardization, manager training, and governance work.

The cost of making the source data reliable was larger than the near-term benefit of AI-generated reporting.

The scale decision was stop.

Not forever.

For now.

The company redirected effort to a more basic management improvement: define reporting standards, decision categories, metric ownership, and escalation rules.

AI could return later as an evidence-preparation layer.

Stopping protected the company from scaling a polished but weak reporting machine.

Lesson

Some AI projects should stop because the workflow is not ready.

That is not failure. It is maturity.

Implementation lesson: If AI exposes that the underlying process lacks ownership, definitions, reliable data, or decision standards, the right answer may be to fix the system first and return to AI later.

Case 6 - The Manufacturing AI Pilot That Could Not Survive the Plant Floor

Setup

A mid-sized manufacturer wanted to use AI to improve quality control and reduce unplanned downtime.

The business case looked obvious. Scrap was expensive. Rework was increasing. Experienced technicians were retiring. Maintenance teams were stretched thin. Production managers wanted earlier warnings before equipment problems became line stoppages.

The company approved an AI pilot for predictive maintenance and defect detection.

The pilot used historical machine data, inspection records, maintenance logs, and quality notes. The first results looked promising. AI detected patterns that were difficult to see manually. The vendor demo showed early-warning signals before certain failures. Leadership saw a possible path to lower downtime, fewer defects, and better production predictability.

The pilot worked in the lab.

The plant floor was different.

Baseline

Before AI, maintenance decisions were based on a mix of scheduled inspections, operator experience, sensor readings, maintenance history, and urgent response when equipment failed.

The production team knew the system was imperfect.

Some failures were caught late. Some defects were detected only after material had already moved downstream. Some maintenance decisions relied heavily on a few experienced people. Data existed, but it was not clean or consistent.

The company believed AI could convert scattered signals into earlier action.

That assumption was reasonable.

But the baseline problem was not only prediction.

It was trust, workflow, and operational response.

AI Intervention

AI was trained to identify equipment patterns that might indicate future failure and to flag possible quality deviations.

In the pilot environment, the system performed well on selected lines and historical cases. It highlighted abnormal vibration patterns, temperature changes, cycle-time shifts, and defect clusters.

The team created an early dashboard.

Green meant normal.

Yellow meant monitor.

Red meant action needed.

Managers liked the simplicity.

Operators were less convinced.

Some alerts appeared during normal production variation. Some warnings came too late. Some recommendations did not account for changeovers, supplier variation, material differences, shift practices, or known machine behavior. Maintenance technicians asked why the AI flagged one machine but ignored another. Quality teams asked whether the signal was strong enough to stop a line.

The AI produced alerts.

The organization had not designed the decision.

Rework Tax

The Rework Tax appeared in several forms:

engineers verifying AI alerts

maintenance teams checking false positives

quality teams investigating weak defect signals

supervisors debating whether to stop production

operators ignoring warnings they did not trust

data teams cleaning inconsistent machine records

managers reviewing why alerts did not match plant-floor reality

The AI did not reduce work at first.

It shifted work to investigation.

That investigation was useful, but it was not yet scalable.

What Went Wrong

The company treated predictive insight as if it automatically created operational value.

It did not.

An AI warning is not a maintenance decision.

A defect signal is not a line-stop decision.

A forecast is not production control.

The missing layer was the Decision Boundary.

The organization had not defined what AI could recommend, who owned the action, what evidence was required, when the line should stop, when maintenance should inspect, and when the signal should be ignored as normal variation.

The data was also weaker than expected. Sensor records, maintenance notes, operator comments, and quality outcomes were not always aligned. AI could find patterns, but the organization could not always explain whether those patterns were operationally meaningful.

The pilot proved possibility.

It did not prove production readiness.

Decision Boundary Redesign

The redesigned workflow separated AI into three lanes.

Monitor lane: AI may flag weak signals for trend review. No immediate production action occurs. Engineers review recurring patterns weekly.

Inspect lane: AI may recommend maintenance inspection when signals cross defined thresholds and supporting evidence exists, such as repeated abnormal readings, prior failure history, quality drift, or operator notes.

Escalation lane: AI must escalate to production leadership when the signal involves safety risk, repeated defect clusters, high-value orders, regulatory quality exposure, or a machine already associated with prior failure patterns.

AI may not independently stop a production line.

AI may not classify a defect as acceptable.

AI may not override operator safety judgment.

AI may not trigger maintenance action without showing the evidence path.

The human owners became clear:

Maintenance owns inspection.

Quality owns defect disposition.

Production owns line-continuation decisions.

Safety owns safety-related stop authority.

AI prepares evidence and recommendations. It does not own the plant.

Revised Economics

The original business case claimed AI would reduce downtime and defects broadly.

The revised economics were more disciplined.

The team separated value into categories:

avoided downtime from earlier inspection

reduced scrap from earlier defect detection

reduced senior technician investigation time after better thresholds

improved root-cause analysis from better evidence packets

fewer unnecessary inspections after false positives were reduced

better handoff between production, maintenance, and quality teams

The project no longer scaled as "AI predicts failures."

It scaled as:

"AI prepares early-warning evidence for defined production, maintenance, and quality decisions, with clear thresholds and human ownership."

That made the business case less flashy and more believable.

Lesson

Manufacturing AI does not fail only because the model is weak.

It often fails because the plant-floor decision system is not ready.

A prediction must become a controlled operational decision before it creates value.

Implementation lesson: In manufacturing, AI should not simply predict problems. It should help production, maintenance, quality, and safety teams decide what to inspect, what to escalate, what to stop, and what to leave alone.

Case 7 - The Customer Service Chatbot That Reduced Tickets and Increased Frustration

Setup

A consumer-facing company wanted to reduce customer service costs.

Support volume was high. Wait times were increasing. Agents were overloaded with repetitive questions. Leadership wanted faster answers, lower ticket volume, and 24/7 customer availability.

The company launched an AI chatbot on its website and inside its customer portal.

The first dashboard looked successful.

Chatbot usage increased. Simple questions were answered quickly. Fewer customers opened human tickets for basic issues. The support queue looked lighter.

Then complaints increased.

Customers were not saying the chatbot never worked.

They were saying it worked until it did not — and when it failed, it trapped them.

Baseline

Before AI, customers reached support through chat, phone, email, and portal tickets.

The process was slow, but customers eventually reached a human.

The biggest support categories included order status, billing questions, account access, returns, service changes, and issue escalation.

Leadership saw a cost problem.

Agents were spending too much time on repetitive questions.

That was true.

But the customer experience problem was more complicated. Customers did not only want fast answers. They wanted resolution, especially when the situation was unusual, emotional, expensive, or time-sensitive.

The baseline problem was not only ticket volume.

It was escalation quality.

AI Intervention

The chatbot handled routine questions.

It answered basic account questions, explained return rules, provided order-status links, summarized policy pages, and guided customers through common steps.

For simple cases, the chatbot helped.

But the company gave the chatbot too much responsibility for containment. The system was designed to reduce human tickets, not to detect when a human was needed.

The chatbot kept trying to solve cases it should have escalated.

A customer with a billing dispute received policy explanations but no resolution path.

A customer with a delayed order kept receiving tracking summaries.

A customer with a locked account was repeatedly told to reset a password even after the reset failed.

A customer trying to cancel a service was sent through multiple loops.

A frustrated customer finally reached a human agent, but the agent received a poor summary and had to ask the customer to repeat the problem.

The ticket count fell.

Customer frustration rose.

Rework Tax

The Rework Tax was hidden in customer experience.

It included:

- customers repeating information after chatbot failure
- agents repairing conversations instead of resolving issues
- escalation summaries that missed emotional or financial context
- supervisors handling complaints from customers who felt blocked
- refunds and credits issued after poor service recovery
- negative reviews caused by containment loops
- support teams manually correcting chatbot knowledge gaps

The dashboard showed fewer tickets.

The business absorbed more frustration.

That is not a clean cost reduction.

That is cost displacement.

What Went Wrong

The company measured deflection, not resolution.

Deflection means the customer did not reach a human.

Resolution means the customer's problem was actually handled.

Those are not the same.

A chatbot that prevents tickets can look efficient while damaging trust.

The missing Decision Boundary was simple:

When should the chatbot stop trying to answer and escalate to a human?

The company had not defined enough escalation triggers.

It had also failed to separate routine informational questions from high-friction service problems.

Decision Boundary Redesign

The redesigned chatbot workflow created four lanes.

Answer lane: AI may answer simple informational questions when the source is approved and the customer's request is low risk.

Guide lane: AI may walk the customer through a standard process, such as checking order status, updating account information, or finding a policy.

Escalate lane: AI must offer human support when the customer shows repeated failure, billing dispute, cancellation intent, account lockout, missing order, legal/compliance language, emotional frustration, medical/financial sensitivity, or repeated negative sentiment.

Stop lane: AI must stop trying to solve the issue when it has failed twice, when the customer asks for a human, when the request affects money or rights, or when the situation falls outside approved support paths.

The chatbot also had to preserve context for the human agent.

A good escalation summary now included:

What the customer wanted.

What the chatbot already tried.

What failed.

What policy or account information was relevant.

Whether the customer was frustrated.

What decision the human agent needed to make next.

AI was no longer measured only by containment.

It was measured by resolution quality.

Revised Economics

The original business case said the chatbot reduced support tickets.

The revised economics were more accurate.

The company measured:

- true resolution rate
- repeat contact rate
- escalation quality
- customer satisfaction after chatbot use
- human-agent handle time after escalation
- refund or credit rate after failed chatbot interactions
- complaint volume
- negative review mentions
- customer retention risk

The chatbot still had value.

It handled routine questions at low cost. It gave customers faster answers for simple issues. It reduced low-value agent workload.

But the company stopped treating every prevented ticket as savings.

A prevented ticket was valuable only if the customer's issue was actually resolved.

The new business case became:

"AI reduces support cost when it resolves routine questions and escalates high-friction cases early enough to protect customer trust."

That is a better standard.

Lesson

Customer service AI should not be designed only to keep people away from humans.

It should be designed to resolve routine issues and recognize when human service is the product.

Implementation lesson: In customer support, the most important chatbot feature may not be the answer. It may be the escalation rule.

Case 8 - The Healthcare Workflow That Improved Speed but Increased Risk

Setup

A regional healthcare organization wanted to reduce pressure on its patient support and care coordination teams.

The goal was not to replace clinicians. Leadership was careful about that. The first AI use case looked administrative: summarize patient messages, prepare prior authorization packets, draft routine follow-up notes, route requests to the right department, and help staff organize information before review.

The business problem was real.

Patients were waiting too long for responses. Staff were overloaded. Nurses, coordinators, billing teams, and front-office employees spent hours each week reading messages, checking records, preparing explanations, and rewriting the same kinds of administrative notes. Managers wanted faster service without adding more people.

The AI pilot looked promising.

Patient message summaries appeared in seconds. Prior authorization packets became easier to prepare. Staff could review long histories more quickly. Routine messages sounded more polished. Internal routing improved at the first step. The dashboard showed faster preparation time.

Then the risk appeared.

The AI was not only helping with paperwork.

It was touching the edge of clinical meaning, privacy, consent, payer access, patient urgency, and accountable communication.

That changed the nature of the workflow.

The organization thought it was implementing an administrative assistant.

In practice, it had built an AI system that could influence healthcare decisions without enough boundaries.

Baseline

Before AI, the workflow was slower but more cautious.

A coordinator might spend 20 to 30 minutes reviewing a patient message, checking appointment history, confirming prior notes, identifying missing forms, and preparing a response or internal handoff. The process was inefficient, but experienced staff knew when to pause.

If the message involved symptoms, medication concerns, treatment timing, privacy, insurance denial language, family-member access, worsening condition, or emotional distress, the staff member usually escalated.

That hesitation had value.

It was not just delay. It was judgment.

The baseline problem was not simply that administrative work took too long. The real problem was that administrative work often carried hidden clinical, privacy, financial, and patient-experience risk.

That is the first healthcare AI secret many teams miss:

In healthcare, the label "administrative" does not automatically mean "low risk."

A scheduling note can reveal urgency.
A billing issue can create care-access risk.
A prior authorization delay can affect treatment timing.
A portal message can begin with a routine question and end with symptoms.
A family request can become a privacy issue.
A simple draft can accidentally sound like medical advice.

The workflow needed speed.

But it needed safer routing even more.

AI Intervention

The AI system summarized patient messages, drafted administrative replies, organized prior authorization support notes, and suggested routing categories.

For clean, routine cases, it helped.

It could summarize a recent appointment history. It could draft a polite reminder. It could identify missing forms. It could help prepare payer-facing documentation. It could reduce the blank-page problem for staff who needed to write a routine message.

The problem appeared in mixed cases.

A patient asked about rescheduling but also mentioned worsening symptoms.
A billing question included language suggesting the patient might delay care because of cost.
A prior authorization packet needed medical necessity language that required clinical review.
A family member requested information, but authorization was unclear.
A patient portal message looked routine until it mentioned medication side effects.
A payer-facing note sounded complete but softened important clinical context.

The AI did not fail because it was useless.

It failed because the organization had not defined where administrative preparation ended and accountable healthcare judgment began.

Rework Tax

The first report claimed the AI reduced preparation time by 40 to 60 percent on selected tasks.

That was only the visible gain.

After the pilot expanded, the hidden Rework Tax appeared.

Staff had to check whether summaries omitted important patient context. Nurses reviewed drafts that should never have been framed as routine replies. Privacy staff corrected assumptions about who could receive information. Billing teams revised payer-facing language. Managers handled escalations when patients felt misunderstood. Clinical staff rechecked AI-prepared summaries before acting. Compliance reviewers asked why certain messages lacked a clear audit trail.

The workflow became faster at producing words.

It became harder at deciding whether those words were safe.

That is the healthcare version of the Rework Tax.

The expensive step is not always drafting. The expensive step is knowing whether a draft is administrative, clinical, privacy-sensitive, payer-sensitive, urgent, or unsafe.

If AI makes that classification unclear, it does not remove work. It moves work to more expensive reviewers.

What Went Wrong

The organization made three mistakes.

First, it treated patient communication as a writing problem.

It was not. It was a decision-routing problem.

Second, it measured speed before measuring escalation accuracy.

A faster response is not an improvement if it misses the signal that should have moved the case to a nurse, physician, privacy officer, billing lead, or supervisor.

Third, it allowed AI to produce confident language in cases where uncertainty should have triggered a stop.

In healthcare, polished language can be dangerous. A message can sound calm, helpful, and professional while still being wrong, incomplete, or outside the sender's authority.

The team needed better questions:

Is this purely administrative?
Does it mention symptoms, medication, diagnosis, treatment, urgency, consent, privacy, payer denial, financial hardship, or patient distress?
Who owns the response?
What must AI never say?
What evidence must be attached?
What requires clinical review?
What requires privacy review?
What requires supervisor escalation?
What must be documented?

The AI system was asked to help the workflow before the workflow had defined the decision boundary.

Decision Boundary Redesign

The redesigned workflow separated the AI role into four lanes.

Administrative preparation lane. AI may summarize appointment history, identify missing forms, prepare routine reminders, organize non-clinical information, and draft simple administrative language for human review.

Clinical-review lane. AI may prepare a summary, but a licensed clinical owner must review anything involving symptoms, diagnosis, medication, treatment, care instructions, medical necessity, or clinical urgency.

Privacy and consent lane. AI must stop when the message involves family members, third-party requests, unclear authorization, sensitive records, identity uncertainty, or disclosure risk.

Escalation lane. AI must escalate when patient language suggests worsening symptoms, medication side effects, delayed care, emotional distress, denied access, complaint risk, legal concern, or uncertainty about the proper owner.

The organization also added a simple rule:

AI may prepare, organize, and suggest.
AI may not independently advise, reassure, deny, disclose, approve, or downgrade risk.

That rule changed the project.

The AI system no longer tried to make healthcare communication merely faster. It helped prepare better evidence for the right human owner.

Clinical staff owned clinical meaning.
Privacy and compliance owned disclosure boundaries.
Billing and authorization teams owned payer workflow.
Care coordinators owned administrative follow-through.
Leadership owned escalation standards.

The secret was not to make AI more aggressive.

The secret was to make AI better at stopping.

Revised Economics

The original business case was too broad:

"AI reduces healthcare administration time."

The revised business case was more accurate:

"AI reduces routine preparation burden while routing clinical, privacy, payer, and patient-risk decisions to the correct accountable owner."

That was less dramatic, but more valuable.

The organization found real gains in narrow, controlled workflows:

faster preparation of routine summaries
fewer incomplete authorization packets
cleaner handoffs to clinical reviewers
better routing of mixed-context patient messages
less time rewriting routine administrative notes
earlier detection of escalation signals
stronger documentation around who reviewed what
lower risk of treating sensitive cases as routine

The AI project became useful when it stopped pretending every message was just a message.

In healthcare, the most important implementation question is not:

Can AI draft this faster?

The better question is:

What kind of decision is hiding inside this communication?

Lesson

Healthcare AI does not become safe because the task is called administrative.

It becomes safer when the organization defines exactly where administrative support ends and accountable human judgment begins.

The strongest healthcare AI implementations do not start by asking AI to "handle more."

They start by teaching the workflow when to stop, escalate, attach evidence, and preserve ownership.

Implementation lesson: In healthcare administration, AI should prepare evidence, summarize context, and reduce routine burden, but it must escalate aggressively when patient safety, clinical meaning, privacy, payer access, consent, or patient rights enter the workflow.

Case 9 - The Venture Portfolio That Confused AI Activity With Enterprise Value

Setup

A venture capital firm wanted its portfolio companies to adopt AI faster.

The logic was reasonable. Investors wanted efficiency. Founders wanted leverage. Operators wanted speed. Board members wanted to know which companies were building durable AI advantage and which were merely falling behind.

Within months, the portfolio looked active.

One company launched an AI sales assistant. Another used AI for customer support. Another added coding tools. Another tested AI for financial reporting. Another created marketing content systems. Another built internal knowledge assistants. Several founders mentioned AI in board updates. A few even said AI had changed how their company worked.

The energy was real.

The evidence was weak.

The firm had many AI stories, but it did not have a reliable way to tell which AI efforts improved enterprise value.

That is the venture capital version of AI Theater.

At company level, AI Theater looks like pilots, dashboards, internal excitement, and tool usage.

At portfolio level, AI Theater looks like every company reporting AI activity while investors struggle to separate useful operating leverage from polished noise.

Baseline

Before the AI push, portfolio companies reported performance through familiar operating metrics: revenue growth, gross margin, burn rate, runway, churn, sales efficiency, customer acquisition cost, support cost, product velocity, net revenue retention, and hiring needs.

Those metrics were imperfect, but they connected to enterprise value.

After the AI push, a new layer of reporting appeared.

Companies reported AI tools adopted, prompts used, hours saved, tickets deflected, content produced, code generated, meetings summarized, and pilots launched.

The problem was not that these signals were useless.

The problem was that they were not comparable.

One founder counted more outbound emails as productivity.
Another counted faster coding as engineering leverage.
Another counted customer-service deflection as cost reduction.
Another counted "hours saved" without explaining what happened to those hours.
Another counted AI-generated content as marketing output, even though pipeline quality did not improve.
Another claimed avoided hiring, but the team had simply pushed review work to senior staff.

The portfolio looked more AI-enabled.

But the firm could not tell which companies were actually becoming more valuable.

That is a dangerous gap for investors.

Venture capital does not need AI enthusiasm. It needs evidence of operating leverage.

AI Intervention

The firm created a portfolio AI initiative.

Each company was asked to identify AI use cases, report early wins, and show where AI could improve efficiency, growth, or execution.

Some use cases were genuinely promising.

A B2B SaaS company used AI to summarize customer success notes and identify churn signals.
A cybersecurity company used AI to prepare analyst summaries.
A healthcare-adjacent company used AI to organize compliance evidence.
A services company used AI to draft proposals.
A marketplace company used AI to route support issues.
An internal finance team used AI to prepare variance explanations.

But the reporting became noisy.

The companies had different incentives, different baselines, different risk levels, and different definitions of success.

One board deck said AI improved productivity by 30 percent. Another said AI reduced support workload by 40 percent. Another said sales teams were moving twice as fast. Another said engineering velocity improved. Another said marketing output increased 300 percent.

The numbers sounded useful.

But the firm could not answer the harder question:

Which of these claims should affect capital allocation, hiring plans, valuation, risk assessment, or follow-on support?

That is where AI activity and enterprise value separated.

Rework Tax

The Rework Tax appeared at two levels.

Inside portfolio companies, teams spent time verifying AI outputs, correcting drafts, reviewing code, handling exceptions, managing customer complaints, cleaning up data, and documenting decisions after the fact.

At the venture firm level, partners and operators spent time interpreting inconsistent AI claims.

Founder time went into preparing AI success narratives.
Operating partners asked for better baselines.
Finance leaders challenged unsupported savings claims.
Customer success teams explained why ticket deflection did not equal better service.
Engineering leaders admitted faster code also created review burden.
Legal and compliance reviewers found that AI workflows had spread before risk review caught up.
Board meetings spent more time discussing AI activity than operating impact.

This is a portfolio-level implementation secret:

AI does not only create Rework Tax inside workflows. It can create Rework Tax inside governance, reporting, and investor decision-making.

When every company describes AI progress differently, the portfolio owner inherits interpretation cost.

The firm was not only evaluating companies.

It was evaluating the quality of each company's AI evidence.

What Went Wrong

The venture firm made a common mistake.

It treated AI adoption as a sign of operational maturity before defining what AI value meant.

The firm did not need every company to use the same tools. That would have been unrealistic.

But it did need a shared standard for evaluating AI impact.

Without that standard, portfolio reporting became a collection of success stories.

The missing questions were simple but uncomfortable:

Did AI improve gross margin or only make work feel faster?
Did it reduce burn or only delay hiring?

Did it improve sales conversion or only increase outreach volume?

Did it reduce churn or only produce better summaries?

Did it improve engineering velocity without increasing defects, rework, or security risk?

Did it reduce support cost without increasing customer frustration?

Did it improve compliance readiness or create new audit exposure?

Did the company count review, correction, exception handling, tool cost, integration cost, and management time?

Can ordinary employees repeat the improvement, or does it depend on one skilled AI champion?

Does this AI workflow make the company more valuable, more defensible, or more efficient?

A founder saying "we are using AI across the company" is not enough.

The better statement is:

"This AI workflow improved this operating metric, after this review burden, inside this boundary, with this owner, and therefore deserves scale."

That is investor-grade AI evidence.

Decision Boundary Redesign

The venture firm redesigned portfolio AI reporting around four categories.

Efficiency AI. These use cases reduce cost per completed unit after review, correction, exceptions, tools, and management time are counted.

Growth AI. These use cases improve qualified pipeline, conversion, expansion, retention, onboarding, activation, sales productivity, or customer success outcomes.

Risk-control AI. These use cases improve compliance readiness, cybersecurity response, audit evidence, fraud detection, service quality, decision traceability, or operational resilience.

Capability AI. These use cases may not yet show financial impact, but they create strategic learning, cleaner data, repeatable workflows, internal skill, or future operating leverage.

This classification helped because it stopped companies from forcing every AI project into fake ROI.

Some projects deserved to be called learning.
Some deserved to be called risk control.
Some deserved to be called efficiency.
Some deserved to be stopped.

The firm also required a compact Evidence Pack for any AI initiative mentioned in a board-level operating review.

The Evidence Pack had to include:

workflow
business decision improved
baseline metric
AI-assisted metric
review burden
exception rate
total cost
risk level
human owner
decision boundary
recommended action: scale, redesign, continue testing, or stop

The firm added one more rule:

Do not report "hours saved" unless you can show what happened to those hours.

Were they converted into lower cost, higher throughput, better quality, faster sales cycles, improved retention, lower support burden, reduced hiring need, or stronger customer experience?

If not, the claim stayed in the category of productivity signal, not enterprise value.

That rule changed the board conversation immediately.

It made weak AI claims harder to hide and strong AI work easier to recognize.

Revised Economics

The revised portfolio view became sharper.

Some AI projects were downgraded.

A content automation project produced more output but did not improve pipeline quality.
A coding assistant improved speed but increased senior review burden.
A chatbot reduced ticket volume but frustrated high-value customers.
A finance automation use case helped with routine classification but failed on exceptions.
A sales automation workflow increased outbound volume but reduced reply quality.

Other projects became stronger.

A customer success workflow identified churn signals earlier and improved account review quality.
A compliance evidence workflow reduced audit-preparation burden.
A support routing workflow improved escalation accuracy.
A proposal-preparation workflow reduced sales-engineer time without weakening quality.
A cybersecurity evidence workflow helped analysts prepare faster without automating risky response decisions.

The firm stopped asking:

Which companies are using AI?

It started asking:

Which AI workflows improve the operating metrics that drive enterprise value?

That changed everything.

AI became less of a theme and more of an operating lens.

The best founders were not the ones with the most AI tools. They were the ones who could explain where AI changed cost structure, customer value, risk posture, or execution speed without hiding the Rework Tax.

Lesson

Venture capital does not need portfolio companies to perform AI sophistication.

It needs proof of AI operating leverage.

A company can use AI everywhere and still fail to improve margin, growth, retention, defensibility, or execution quality. Another company can use AI in three narrow workflows and create real value because those workflows connect directly to enterprise value drivers.

The venture secret is this:

AI should not be evaluated by how modern a company sounds. It should be evaluated by whether it changes the company's economic engine.

Implementation lesson: For venture capital, private equity, boards, and portfolio operators, AI should be evaluated by its effect on enterprise value drivers — margin, growth, retention, risk, defensibility, execution quality, and operating leverage — not by adoption activity alone.

Case 10 - The Procurement Agent That Saved Time and Created Vendor-Risk Exposure

Setup

A mid-sized company wanted to modernize procurement.

The procurement team was overloaded with vendor emails, internal purchase requests, contract renewals, pricing comparisons, invoice questions, and routine approval follow-ups. Business units complained that procurement was too slow. Finance complained that requests were incomplete. IT complained that software purchases were appearing outside approved channels. Legal complained that contracts arrived too late for review.

The company did not begin with a reckless goal. It did not ask AI to sign contracts or approve large purchases without oversight.

The first goal sounded practical:

Use AI to help employees prepare purchase requests, compare vendor responses, summarize contract terms, flag missing information, and route routine requests to the right reviewer.

The pilot looked successful.

Request preparation became faster. Vendor emails were summarized quickly. Procurement staff spent less time chasing missing details. Internal users liked the assistant because it helped them explain what they wanted to buy. Managers liked the cleaner intake forms. Finance liked the idea of fewer incomplete requests.

Then the risk appeared.

The AI system was not only helping people prepare requests.

It was beginning to shape which vendors looked safer, cheaper, faster, and easier to approve.

That changed the nature of the workflow.

The company thought it had built a procurement assistant.

In practice, it had built an early-stage procurement decision system.

Baseline

Before AI, the procurement process was slow but familiar.

An employee submitted a request. Procurement checked vendor information, pricing, business justification, budget alignment, security review status, payment terms, legal requirements, and approval authority. Finance reviewed spend. IT reviewed technology and data exposure. Legal reviewed contracts when needed.

The process frustrated people because it created delays.

But those delays had a purpose.

Procurement was not only buying things. It was protecting the company from bad vendors, duplicate tools, weak contracts, hidden subscriptions, security exposure, payment fraud, budget leakage, and unmanaged commitments.

The baseline workflow had a speed problem.

It also had a control function.

That distinction mattered.

If AI only reduced delay, it could help.

If AI weakened control, it could create a larger problem than the one it solved.

AI Intervention

The AI assistant helped employees draft purchase requests and organize vendor information.

It summarized proposals. It extracted renewal dates. It compared pricing language. It identified missing documents. It drafted internal justification notes. It suggested routing based on vendor type, dollar amount, department, and category.

For simple requests, the system helped.

A routine software renewal became easier to prepare. A small office equipment purchase moved faster. A repeat vendor request required fewer back-and-forth emails. Procurement staff could review cleaner submissions.

The problem appeared in the gray zone.

A vendor looked like a routine software supplier but required access to customer data.
A low-cost tool carried auto-renewal terms that created long-term spend.
A department requested a "small" AI tool that connected to internal documents.
A vendor changed bank details during an active invoice cycle.
A contract summary missed an indemnity limitation.
A purchasing request looked operational but created compliance exposure.
A vendor comparison emphasized price while underweighting security and exit risk.

The AI assistant did not intend to create risk.

It simply optimized the wrong surface.

It made procurement look faster before the company defined which procurement decisions were allowed to move faster.

Rework Tax

The early dashboard showed shorter intake time and faster request preparation.

But the hidden cost appeared after review.

Procurement staff had to recheck AI summaries for missing contract terms.
Finance had to verify whether savings claims were real or just shifted into longer commitments.
IT had to review tools that had been described too casually as "low risk."
Security had to investigate vendors after departments had already become interested.
Legal had to correct AI-generated contract summaries that sounded complete but missed important exposure.
Managers had to explain why some "AI-recommended" vendors were not approved.
Accounts payable had to verify vendor changes more carefully because the AI system made email summaries look cleaner than the underlying risk.

The Rework Tax was not only time.

It was confidence correction.

Once an AI-generated summary framed a vendor as cheaper, faster, or lower risk, reviewers had to work harder to challenge that framing.

That is a subtle but serious cost.

AI did not merely summarize procurement information.

It influenced procurement judgment.

What Went Wrong

The organization treated procurement as an administrative workflow.

That was the mistake.

Procurement contains administrative work, but it also contains financial control, vendor-risk management, cybersecurity review, contract discipline, data governance, budget protection, and fraud prevention.

The AI assistant was helpful at preparing information.

It was weaker at knowing when information became a decision.

The company failed to define the boundary between:

preparing a request
summarizing a vendor
comparing options
recommending a vendor
approving a purchase
changing payment details
accepting contract terms
allowing data access
creating a long-term obligation

These are not the same decision.

A tool that can assist with the first three should not automatically influence the last five.

The company also measured the wrong success signal. It measured request speed, not control quality.

The better questions were:

Did AI reduce incomplete requests without increasing risky approvals?

Did it reduce procurement cycle time without bypassing finance, IT, security, or legal review?

Did it identify vendor risk earlier?

Did it prevent duplicate tools?

Did it improve budget discipline?

Did it catch contract and renewal exposure?

Did it reduce fraud risk or make suspicious changes look more polished?

Did it improve total cost of ownership, or only make the intake process smoother?

Without those questions, the company was measuring convenience while ignoring exposure.

Decision Boundary Redesign

The redesigned procurement workflow separated AI into five roles.

Request preparation: AI may help employees describe the business need, collect required details, identify missing information, and prepare a cleaner intake form.

Vendor summarization: AI may summarize proposals, pricing, renewal dates, contract terms, support commitments, data-access requirements, and implementation assumptions — but summaries must include source references and uncertainty flags.

Risk flagging: AI may flag possible concerns, including customer-data access, sensitive integrations, unusual payment requests, auto-renewal terms, high switching costs, weak cancellation rights, unclear liability language, or vendor bank-detail changes.

Recommendation support: AI may compare options using approved criteria, but it may not select the vendor alone. Human owners must review cost, risk, business fit, and strategic need.

Stop and escalate: AI must stop when the request involves new vendor bank details, access to sensitive data, regulated information, customer records, security tooling, AI tools connected to internal knowledge, unusual contract terms, large commitments, executive exceptions, or unclear approval authority.

The ownership model became explicit.

Procurement owns process quality.
Finance owns budget and payment control.
IT owns technical fit and system access.
Security owns vendor and data-risk review.
Legal owns contract exposure.
The business unit owns the business need.
Leadership owns exceptions.

AI became useful after it stopped behaving like a quiet approver.

Revised Economics

The revised business case became more credible.

The company no longer claimed:

"AI reduces procurement time by 50 percent."

That was too broad.

The better claim was:

"AI reduces procurement intake friction and improves request completeness for routine purchases, while escalating vendor-risk, payment-risk, data-risk, and contract-risk decisions to the correct human owners."

That claim was less glamorous.

It was also safer and more valuable.

The organization found that AI created real gains in specific areas:

fewer incomplete purchase requests
faster preparation of routine renewals
cleaner vendor comparison packets
earlier identification of missing security information
better visibility into auto-renewals and duplicate tools
less time spent rewriting employee justifications
more consistent routing to finance, IT, legal, and security
reduced risk of treating sensitive vendor requests as routine purchases

The strongest value did not come from autonomous purchasing.

It came from better procurement evidence.

AI helped the organization move faster because the human review layer received cleaner, more complete, better-routed information.

That is implementation.

Not replacing control.

Strengthening it.

Lesson

Procurement AI is dangerous when it is treated as simple paperwork automation.

Procurement is where cost, contracts, vendors, data access, fraud risk, security exposure, and long-term obligations meet.

AI can help prepare requests, summarize options, and expose missing information. But it should not quietly become the decision-maker for vendor trust, payment changes, contract acceptance, or risk approval.

Implementation lesson: In procurement and vendor management, AI should accelerate evidence preparation, not weaken control. The more an AI system influences vendor selection, payment, data access, or contract obligations, the stronger the decision boundary must become.

Closing Note

These cases show the same pattern in different systems.

AI looked useful at the surface. The first output improved. Activity increased. The pilot looked promising.

But the real business question appeared only after review, ownership, exception handling, decision boundaries, and economics were counted.

That is the central discipline of this book.

AI implementation is not the art of making software do more.

It is the discipline of making business systems decide better.

Part VI - The Decision Architect's Toolkit

Practical Tools for Turning AI Strategy Into Implementation Discipline

This toolkit is intentionally compact.

The purpose is not to turn this book into a workbook. The purpose is to give leaders, consultants, operators, AI strategists, and implementation teams a usable set of tools they can apply immediately.

Extended worksheets, editable templates, calculators, and expanded examples can live in the Companion Implementation Kit. The book version should stay focused, practical, and readable.

Use these tools in sequence when possible:

Diagnose the workflow.
Measure the hidden cost.
Define the boundary.
Test the pilot.
Build the evidence.
Decide whether to scale, redesign, continue testing, or stop.

Tool 1 - AI Readiness Audit

The AI Readiness Audit helps determine whether a workflow is ready for AI implementation or only ready for exploration.

Do not begin by asking whether the tool is powerful. Begin by asking whether the business system is ready to use the tool responsibly.

A workflow is AI-ready when five conditions are reasonably clear.

First, the workflow is specific. "Use AI in operations" is too broad. "Use AI to prepare exception packets for delayed supplier shipments" is specific enough to evaluate.

Second, the decision is visible. AI should support a decision such as classify, route, escalate, approve, draft, investigate, prioritize, or stop.

Third, the data is usable. If key information is missing, outdated, scattered, inconsistent, or trapped in informal conversations, AI may generate polished uncertainty.

Fourth, ownership is named. A tool owner is not enough. The workflow needs a business owner who is accountable for the outcome.

Fifth, value can be measured. The team should be able to identify at least one operating metric: cycle time, rework, review burden, cost per unit, escalation accuracy, conversion, retention, audit readiness, or risk reduction.

Use this audit before pilots, vendor selection, or scale decisions.

Ask:

What workflow are we improving?
What decision does AI support?
What data does the decision require?
Who owns the outcome?
What can go wrong if AI is wrong?
What evidence would prove improvement?
What should AI not do here?

A workflow does not need to be perfect to begin testing. But if the team cannot answer these questions, the project is not ready for scale.

It may still be worth exploring. It is not yet implementation-ready.

Use this tool when: a team proposes a new AI use case, tool purchase, pilot, or automation idea.

Decision output: ready to test, redesign first, explore only, or stop.

Tool 2 - Rework Tax Calculator

The Rework Tax Calculator prevents fake productivity math.

AI often makes the first output faster. That does not mean the completed workflow is faster. The hidden cost appears in verification, correction, exception handling, and review.

Use this formula:

Net Gain = (Baseline Time − AI-Assisted Time) − (Verification + Correction + Exception Handling)

Baseline Time is how long the workflow took before AI.

AI-Assisted Time is how long the AI-assisted first version takes.

Verification is the time spent checking the output.

Correction is the time spent fixing the output.

Exception Handling is the time spent managing cases AI cannot complete, misroutes, misunderstands, or makes uncertain.

This calculator should be applied to real cases, not ideal examples. Start with 25 cases if volume is limited. Use 50 or 100 if the workflow is high-volume.

Do not average routine and high-risk exceptions too early. Separate them if possible.

A workflow may show strong gains for routine cases and weak gains for exceptions. That is useful. It tells you where AI fits and where it needs stronger boundaries.

Example:
Baseline Time: 30 minutes
AI-Assisted Time: 8 minutes

Verification: 7 minutes

Correction: 4 minutes

Exception Handling: 5 minutes

Net Gain $= (30 - 8) - (7 + 4 + 5)$

Net Gain $= 22 - 16$

Net Gain $= 6$ minutes

The project still helps, but not by 22 minutes. It helps by 6 minutes after hidden work is counted.

That difference matters for ROI.

Use this tool when: a team claims AI "saved time."

Decision output: real gain, weak gain, no gain, or negative gain.

Tool 3 - Real Velocity Calculator

The Real Velocity Calculator measures how fast the organization actually moves after delayed errors and cleanup are counted.

AI can create an output quickly, but the cost of mistakes may arrive later. This is especially important in cybersecurity, finance, support, operations, legal review, and customer-facing workflows.

Use this formula:

Real Velocity $=$ AI Output Speed $-$ (Detection Latency $+$ Rework Time)

AI Output Speed is the visible speed improvement.

Detection Latency is the time it takes to notice that something is wrong, incomplete, risky, misleading, or misrouted.

Rework Time is the time required to fix the issue.

This tool matters because not all AI errors are detected immediately. A weak ticket classification may not be noticed until a customer complains. A misleading sales follow-up may not be noticed until the deal stalls. A bad finance classification may not appear until audit cleanup. A weak security summary may not matter until related alerts appear later.

Use this calculator when the cost of being wrong is delayed.

Ask:

How quickly does AI create the output?

How quickly would we detect a wrong output?

Who detects it?

How expensive is correction?

Does the correction happen before or after customer, financial, security, compliance, or operational impact?

Can the workflow surface errors earlier?

If Detection Latency is high, do not scale automation. Redesign the workflow so uncertainty, missing evidence, and exception triggers appear earlier.

Real Velocity is not about making AI slower.

It is about preventing false speed.

Use this tool when: errors may appear downstream or after the workflow has moved forward.

Decision output: safe acceleration, delayed-risk workflow, redesign required, or stop.

Tool 4 - Decision Boundary Matrix

The Decision Boundary Matrix defines what AI may do, what humans must own, and where the system must stop.

Do not define AI's role for an entire department. Define it for one decision at a time.

Start with the decision type.

Deterministic decisions follow clear rules: thresholds, required-field matches, routing rules, duplicate checks, or approved categories. AI can usually assist or recommend. It may act only when risk is low, the rule is clear, and the outcome is easy to monitor.

Probabilistic decisions involve likelihood, pattern recognition, or confidence rather than certainty. AI can usually assist. It may recommend, but review is normally required before the workflow changes. AI should rarely act alone unless the case is narrow, low-risk, and monitored.

Judgment-based decisions require business context, ethics, legal interpretation, customer nuance, security responsibility, reputation, or executive accountability. AI can assist by preparing evidence, summaries, comparisons, or options. Humans must own the decision.

For each decision, assign one role:

Assist: AI prepares information.
Recommend: AI suggests a path.
Act: AI performs a narrow approved action.
Escalate: AI sends the case to the right human owner.
Stop: AI blocks the next step until review occurs.

Use this compact decision statement:

AI may ___________ when ___________.
AI must escalate when ___________.
AI must stop when ___________.
The human owner is ___________.

Example:

AI may recommend routine invoice status when vendor, amount, purchase order, approval path, and payment details match approved records. AI must escalate when payment details change, vendor data is missing, or duplicate signals appear. AI must stop before payment approval. The human owner is finance operations.

Use this tool when: AI influences routing, classification, approval, prioritization, communication, or action.

Decision output: assist, recommend, act, escalate, or stop.

Tool 5 - Workflow Mapping Template

The Workflow Mapping Template reveals the decisions hidden inside the work.

A process map often shows steps. A useful AI workflow map shows decisions.

Use this sequence:

Trigger: What starts the workflow?
Actors: Who touches it?
Decision points: What decisions move it forward?
Evidence: What information is needed at each decision?
Exceptions: Where does the normal path break?
Outcome: What does "done" mean?
Owner: Who is accountable for the outcome?
AI role: Where can AI assist, recommend, act, escalate, or stop?

Do not accept vague verbs such as review, process, handle, manage, or assess. Push until the decision is visible.

Instead of:

"Review the ticket."

Write:

"Decide whether the ticket is routine, urgent, security-sensitive, or escalation-required."

Instead of:

"Prepare campaign content."

Write:

"Decide which buyer problem, proof point, claim, and next action should shape this campaign."

Instead of:

"Process invoice."

Write:

"Decide whether this invoice is routine, exception, high-risk, or blocked."

The map should also show what AI must not do. This prevents drift. AI may summarize a ticket, but that does not mean it may downgrade a security-sensitive issue. AI may extract invoice fields, but that does not mean it may approve payment. AI may draft a campaign brief, but that does not mean it may invent proof.

A good workflow map is not decorative. It should help the organization decide where AI can improve the system without hiding risk.

Use this tool when: a workflow seems ready for automation but the decisions are not yet clear.

Decision output: mapped workflow, named decisions, evidence needs, exception points, and AI role options.

Tool 6 - What NOT to Automate Checklist

The What NOT to Automate Checklist protects the organization from applying AI where the workflow is not ready.

Do not automate a workflow simply because the tool can do something impressive.

Do not automate when the decision is unclear.

Do not automate when ownership is missing.

Do not automate when required data is unreliable.

Do not automate when the workflow depends on informal expert judgment that has not been mapped.

Do not automate high-risk decisions before review, audit trails, escalation rules, and stop conditions are defined.

Do not automate customer-facing promises when proof, pricing, legal terms, or service commitments are not controlled.

Do not automate financial approvals involving changed payment details, new vendors, unusual amounts, missing purchase orders, duplicate signals, or rushed payment requests.

Do not automate cybersecurity downgrades, containment decisions, or incident response actions unless the action is narrow, approved, tested, monitored, and reversible where possible.

Do not automate healthcare, legal, compliance, HR, or regulated decisions without role clarity and professional oversight.

Do not automate a weak process before deciding whether the process should be redesigned.

This checklist does not say "avoid AI."

It says do not use AI to hide business confusion.

Many workflows are good candidates for AI assistance, evidence preparation, summarization, classification support, drafting, or exception detection. That is different from automation.

When in doubt, move one level down:

From act to recommend.
From recommend to assist.
From assist to evidence preparation.
From evidence preparation to workflow redesign.

The safest AI strategy is not the slowest one. It is the one that matches AI authority to business risk.

Use this tool when: a team wants AI to act, approve, send, route, close, downgrade, or decide.

Decision output: automate, recommend only, assist only, redesign first, or stop.

Tool 7 - Pilot Scorecard

The Pilot Scorecard helps decide whether an AI pilot deserves scale.

Do not score a pilot by enthusiasm alone. Score it by evidence.

Use seven categories.

Workflow clarity: Was the workflow specific enough to test?
Decision clarity: Was the AI-supported decision named?
Baseline quality: Did the team measure the pre-AI workflow?
Boundary quality: Was AI's role clear?
Rework impact: Did review, correction, and exception handling remain manageable?
Risk control: Were escalation and stop rules effective?
Economic logic: Did the pilot connect to cost, capacity, revenue, margin, or risk-adjusted value?

For each category, assign a simple rating:

Strong.
Acceptable.
Weak.
Unknown.

Avoid false precision. The scorecard is not meant to create a fake mathematical grade. It is meant to expose weak evidence.

A pilot with several "unknown" ratings is not ready to scale.

A pilot with strong workflow clarity but weak economics may need redesign.

A pilot with good user response but poor boundary control may need risk redesign.

A pilot with strong evidence and manageable cost may deserve production planning.

Every scorecard should end with one recommendation:

Scale.

Redesign.

Continue testing with one specific question.

Stop.

The most important rule: "Continue testing" must name the unanswered question.

Good: "Continue testing to determine whether ordinary users can repeat the result without expert supervision."

Weak: "Continue testing because this seems promising."

The scorecard protects the organization from pilot drift.

Use this tool when: a pilot has finished or is asking for expansion.

Decision output: scale, redesign, continue testing with one question, or stop.

Tool 8 - Executive AI Evidence Pack

The Executive AI Evidence Pack is the short proof file leadership needs before approving scale.

It should not be a long report. It should be clear enough for an executive, CFO, risk leader, or board member to understand quickly.

Include these elements:

Use case: What AI initiative is being evaluated?
Workflow: What business workflow does it affect?
Decision: What decision does AI support?
AI role: Assist, recommend, act, escalate, or stop?
Baseline: What happened before AI?
AI-assisted result: What changed?
Net gain: What improvement remains after review, correction, and exception handling?
Risk level: Low, medium, or high?
Boundary: What is AI allowed and not allowed to do?
Evidence: What records, sources, logs, or approvals are preserved?
Economics: What financial path applies: cost reduction, capacity expansion, revenue improvement, margin protection, or risk-adjusted value?

Production cost: What changes at scale?

Recommendation: Scale, redesign, continue testing, or stop.

The Evidence Pack should include one plain-language executive statement:

"This initiative should / should not scale because ___________."

Example:

"This initiative should scale only for low-risk support ticket triage because it reduced routine classification time without increasing reopen rate, but security-sensitive and executive-user tickets still require escalation."

This is the kind of sentence executives can use.

The Evidence Pack turns AI from a story into a decision.

Use this tool when: an AI project needs executive approval, budget, scale, or governance review.

Decision output: an executive-ready scale-or-stop recommendation.

Tool 9 - 30-60-90 Implementation Plan

The 30-60-90 Implementation Plan helps teams move from interest to disciplined execution.

Do not use this plan for every AI idea. Use it for a workflow that passed the readiness audit and deserves a serious pilot.

First 30 Days: Diagnose and Design

Map the workflow.

Name the decision.

Identify the owner.

Define the risk level.

Assess data readiness.

Write the Decision Boundary.

Define what AI may assist, recommend, act on, escalate, or stop.

Choose success metrics and stop conditions.

Select real cases for testing, including routine, messy, and high-risk cases.

The first 30 days should produce clarity, not dashboards.

Days 31–60: Pilot and Measure

Run the pilot on real workflow cases.

Measure baseline versus AI-assisted performance.

Track verification, correction, exception handling, review burden, and user behavior.

Check whether ordinary users can follow the workflow.

Record where AI output creates trust, confusion, speed, or rework.

Begin the Evidence Pack.

Do not expand scope during this phase unless the original test question is answered.

Days 61–90: Decide and Prepare for Scale

Review the Evidence Pack.

Calculate net gain and real velocity where relevant.

Assess risk, cost, integration needs, governance, training, logging, and ownership.

Make one decision:

Scale.
Redesign.
Continue testing with one specific question.
Stop.

If scaling, prepare the production plan: owner, users, workflow rules, monitoring, escalation, audit trail, cost controls, and review cadence.

The 90-day goal is not "AI transformation."

The goal is one disciplined implementation decision.

Use this tool when: a promising use case is ready for structured testing.

Decision output: scale, redesign, continue testing, or stop after 90 days.

Tool 10 - Shadow Ledger Audit Checklist

The Shadow Ledger Audit Checklist identifies where AI is influencing decisions without ownership, boundaries, or audit trails.

The Shadow Ledger is the untracked record of operational liability created when AI influences decisions without ownership, boundary rules, or audit trails.

Use this checklist on any workflow where AI output affects customers, money, risk, compliance, security, operations, employees, or executive decisions.

Ask:

Does AI influence what gets approved, sent, paid, escalated, classified, prioritized, investigated, promised, rejected, or ignored?

Is there a named human owner?

Is the AI role documented?

Is the risk level defined?

Is there a written boundary?

Is the evidence visible?

Is the reason for the recommendation understandable?

Are exceptions escalated?

Are high-risk cases separated from routine cases?

Is the final decision logged?

Can the organization explain later what happened and who approved it?

If the answer is no to several of these questions, the Shadow Ledger is growing.

Do not treat this as a compliance exercise only. It is also an operating discipline. Shadow Ledger risk often appears later as customer complaints, audit gaps, disputes, rework, financial errors, security misses, or executive uncertainty.

The goal is not to remove AI from the workflow.

The goal is to make AI influence visible.

Start with the highest-risk workflows: payment approvals, customer commitments, cybersecurity triage, healthcare administration, legal language, compliance-sensitive communication, HR decisions, and executive reporting.

The higher the consequence, the stronger the record must be.

Use this tool when: AI influences decisions but ownership or evidence is unclear.

Decision output: acceptable control, boundary redesign, audit trail required, escalation required, or stop.

Part VI Closing Note

The tools in this section are deliberately compact.

They are not meant to replace professional judgment, legal review, financial analysis, cybersecurity governance, healthcare compliance, or operational leadership. They are meant to create a practical starting point.

Use them to ask better questions.

Use them to expose hidden cost.

Use them to prevent weak pilots from drifting.

Use them to protect human judgment.

Use them to decide where AI deserves scale and where it does not.

The best AI implementation systems are not the ones with the most tools.

They are the ones with the clearest decisions.

Final Thoughts - Discipline Over Hype

AI is powerful enough to create real business value.

It is also powerful enough to create confusion faster than organizations can recognize it.

That is the central tension of this book.

The future will not reward companies that merely adopt the most tools, launch the most pilots, generate the most content, or announce the most AI initiatives. Those activities may create motion, but motion is not the same as progress.

The future will reward organizations that can connect AI to real workflows, real decisions, real ownership, real evidence, real economics, and real risk control.

That is the difference between AI activity and AI implementation.

The blind spots described in this book are not abstract. They show up in ordinary business language:

"We saved time."

"The pilot worked."

"The tool is approved."

"AI only recommends."

"A human is still in the loop."

"The output looks good."

"We are moving fast."

Each sentence may be true.

Each sentence may also hide the real question.

Saved time after what review?

Worked under what conditions?

Approved for what decision?

Recommends with what evidence?

Which human, with what authority?

Looks good compared to what standard?

Moving fast toward what outcome?

That is the work of the Decision Architect.

Not to slow AI down for the sake of caution.

Not to create bureaucracy.

Not to turn every experiment into a committee.

The work is to make AI useful inside real business systems.

Useful means the workflow improves.

Useful means the decision is clearer.

Useful means ownership is visible.

Useful means risk is bounded.

Useful means economics are honest.

Useful means weak projects can stop.

Useful means strong projects can scale with confidence.

This is discipline over hype.

AI should not be treated as magic.

It should not be treated as theater.

It should not be treated as a shortcut around management responsibility.

AI should be treated as a powerful capability that must be designed into the business with care.

That is how speed becomes value.

That is how pilots become production.

That is how tools become strategy.

That is how trust becomes structure.

That is how AI implementation becomes real.

The first implementation law of this book still holds:

Speed without boundaries creates cost.

The final lesson is just as important:

AI does not replace business discipline.

It rewards it.

Companion Resources

This book is designed as a practical field manual.

Some readers will want deeper worksheets, editable templates, calculators, scorecards, expanded case studies, workshop materials, implementation prompts, and companion exercises.

The extended Companion Implementation Kit may include:

AI Readiness Audit worksheet

Rework Tax Calculator

Real Velocity Calculator

Decision Boundary Matrix

Workflow Mapping Template

What NOT to Automate Checklist

Pilot Scorecard

Executive AI Evidence Pack template

30-60-90 Implementation Plan

Shadow Ledger Audit Checklist

Scale-or-Stop Review Template

Boardroom AI Readiness worksheet

Industry-specific implementation prompts

Consultant and AI Strategist delivery templates

Extended MSP, cybersecurity, marketing, finance, and operations case studies

These companion materials are intended to help readers apply the book inside real organizations.

They are not required to understand the book.

They are designed for readers who want to move from reading to implementation.

For current companion materials and updates, visit:

AiStrategyService.com

Dedication

To my wife, who helped at every step of this book — including the invisible steps that never appear in the table of contents.
Thank you for your patience, your grammar rescue missions, your honest reactions to too many book-cover versions, and your heroic tolerance of my "quick questions" that somehow became full editorial meetings.
This book is better because you stayed with me through the drafts, the doubts, the corrections, and the covers.

With love and gratitude.

Acknowledgments

This book was written for the people who must make AI work after the demo ends.

For the operations leaders who have to deal with the handoffs.
For the support teams who know when a ticket is more complicated than it looks.
For the cybersecurity analysts who understand that a short summary is not the same as response readiness.
For the finance leaders who ask the uncomfortable but necessary question: "Where does the value show up?"
For the marketers and sales teams who know that more content is not the same as more trust.
For the consultants, founders, MSP leaders, and AI strategists trying to help organizations adopt AI without turning every conversation into hype.
For the executives who want innovation, but also need accountability.
For the professionals who are willing to say yes when the evidence is strong, no when the project is weak, and not yet when the system is not ready.

This book is also for the readers who believe that AI can be useful without being exaggerated.

That is the audience worth writing for.

About the Author

Nikolay Gul is an author, AI strategist, cybersecurity marketing specialist, and founder of Future-Proof Marketing Press.

His work focuses on practical AI implementation, cybersecurity decision-making, high-tech marketing, business strategy, and the intersection of technology, trust, and operational execution. He writes for business leaders, consultants, MSPs, cybersecurity teams, founders, marketers, and professionals who want to use AI without falling into hype, shallow automation, or tool-first thinking.

Nikolay's books and frameworks are built around a consistent principle: technology becomes valuable only when it improves real decisions.

His work emphasizes clarity, trust, measurable value, practical implementation, and decision-first strategy.

His previous publications include work on AI-driven cybersecurity and high-tech marketing, book self-publishing with AI assistance, AI prompting intelligence, cybersecurity buying decisions, and visual AI systems.

Through Future-Proof Marketing Press, Nikolay develops books, field manuals, AI frameworks, and strategic resources designed to help professionals think more clearly about AI adoption, cybersecurity services, marketing execution, and business transformation.

He is based in Syracuse, New York.

For current author information, companion resources, and related publications, visit:

NikolayGul.com
AiStrategyService.com

Source Notes

This book uses selected public research and industry commentary to support one practical argument: AI adoption and AI implementation are not the same thing.

The sources below should be read as context, not as universal proof that AI succeeds or fails in every organization. AI market data, vendor claims, adoption statistics, regulation, cybersecurity expectations, healthcare rules, procurement practices, and investment standards change quickly. Readers should verify current information before relying on any specific external claim for legal, financial, cybersecurity, healthcare, compliance, procurement, investment, or board-level decisions.

Gartner agentic AI cancellation prediction

Gartner reported in June 2025 that more than 40 percent of agentic AI projects would be canceled by the end of 2027 because of escalating costs, unclear business value, or inadequate risk controls. Gartner also described many current agentic AI projects as early-stage experiments or proofs of concept, often driven by hype or misapplied use cases.

This book uses that prediction carefully. It should not be read as proof that agentic AI has no future. It should be read as a warning that agentic AI projects require clear business value, workflow redesign, production economics, ownership, risk controls, and scale discipline before broad deployment.

Source: Gartner Newsroom, "Gartner Predicts Over 40% of Agentic AI Projects Will Be Canceled by End of 2027," June 25, 2025.

MIT NANDA / The GenAI Divide

The MIT NANDA report, *The GenAI Divide: State of AI in Business 2025*, examined the gap between enterprise AI experimentation and measurable business transformation. The report has been widely discussed for its finding that only a small share of integrated AI pilots were extracting major value, while many remained without measurable profit-and-loss impact.

This book uses that framing as a caution about the difference between tool usage and business implementation. The useful lesson is not that AI cannot create value. The useful lesson is that value depends on workflow fit, contextual learning, integration, measurement, ownership, and business alignment.

Source: MIT NANDA, *The GenAI Divide: State of AI in Business 2025*, July 2025.

IDC / Lenovo pilot-to-production reporting

CIO reported on IDC research undertaken with Lenovo, noting that 88 percent of observed AI proof-of-concept projects did not reach wide-scale deployment.

This book uses that reporting to support the Pilot Trap argument: a successful pilot does not automatically prove production readiness. A pilot should produce evidence strong enough to support one of four decisions: scale, redesign, continue testing, or stop.

Source: CIO, "88% of AI pilots fail to reach production — but that's not all on IT," March 25, 2025.

McKinsey AI adoption and scaling research

McKinsey's 2025 AI research emphasizes that capturing value from AI depends on more than adoption. It points to the importance of strategy, operating model, workflow redesign, talent, data, technology, adoption, and scaling practices.

This book uses that research direction as support for its central argument: AI value depends less on tool access alone and more on disciplined implementation inside real business systems.

Source: McKinsey & Company, "The State of AI: Global Survey 2025" and related AI research.

How these sources are used

The external sources in this book should be read as warning signals and strategic context, not as fear marketing.

They should not be reduced to:

"AI is failing."
"Most AI projects are doomed."
"Agentic AI has no future."
"AI adoption is fake."

The more accurate lesson is:

AI adoption is broad, but measurable business value depends on workflow redesign, decision ownership, risk control, evidence, implementation discipline, and financial translation.

That is the discipline this book is built around.